Write them Right

How to Write Effective Letters, Job Applications,
Curricula Vitae, and Take Interviews

Elitham B Turya *MB, MSc.*

A writer on communication skills, and a consultant in child health.

Beihireyo
Books

Beihireyo Books

- P O Box 118, Sale, Cheshire, England M33 4UB.
- P O Box 9959, Kampala, Uganda.

First published by Beihireyo Books 1992,

Copyright (C) E B Turya, 1992, 1996

2nd Edition 1996

ISBN   0 - 9515819 - 5- 3

PREFACE (Dedication)

My dear niece/ nephew,

Several years ago you asked me for advice on writing applications. I wrote and sent you notes on how I communicate in writing.

I have looked at the notes again. I agree with you. They no longer meet your needs. I have revised them and added topics relevant to your current and (hopefully) future needs. These notes are still based on the way I write my private and business communications.

I think hard before making applications. I examine prospective jobs and courses for immediate and future benefits. Will it hasten the attainment of my career goals and/or improve my finances?

Think carefully before applying for a job or a training course. Do you really need it? Will it enhance your career options?

The revised notes include the following:

- Choosing a career
- Making applications
- Writing curricula vitae
- Taking interviews

- Writing letters
- Writing research paper
- Writing dissertations
- Writing reports.

I have used fictitious names (for people), events and addresses, to tell a story. Names of well known institutions are used to maintain a sense of reality.

I hope the notes, and *Further Readings* will be useful in your search for exciting careers. I know you will succeed.

Your uncle

EBJurya

3

Thank you Eva, Grace, and Daudi, for a critical reading of the text.

Glossary

gombolola = an administrative area, a subcounty *(in Uganda)*
mandazi = type of pastry sold by street boys
muramba = an alcoholic drink made of sorghum, millet or maize
Primary 1 = first year of primary education [P.1-7]
S.1 = first year of secondary education [S.1-6]
shamba = small farm, piece of agricultural land
waragi = a gin made from fermented ripe banana juice

4

Contents

4.0   Write Your Curriculum Vitae

5.0 Making Applications

6.0 Taking Interviews

1 Introduction

1 Introduction

Effective communication is essential for success in business and professional life. If I need a job I look *(hunt, search)* for one. I inform prospective employers of my skills, qualifications, suitability and availability. It is my duty.

Even when services are free, the articulate quickly get their share. The inarticulate may not even claim their entitlements. If you are wronged, you need to complain effectively to get redress or compensation.

In complex societies you must be able to write, talk and listen well. *(To win you must play by the rules of the communications game).* To get your story heard, your needs attended to, to influence the community, requires effective communication.

Communication may be achieved in many different ways. This book concentrates on the written message.

Selling your skills
When you apply for a job, or a course of training, your aim is to convince the recruiter to pick you and not somebody else.

You act like a stall holder in a market who displays his wares to customers. The best goods sell first. Similarly the best candidates are selected. Your duty is to present yourself as the best available. Your qualifications, skills, experience and personality, [YOU] are on sale. **You Are the Merchandise and the Merchant (vendor).**

INTRODUCTION

1.2 Career maps

In order to get from one place to another you need a plan of the route -a map. This map may be simple (already in your brain), or complex. Directions to a future career are not readily available. Where do you get career maps from?

You don't know? Have you talked with those whose career you admire? Have you read books on your ambition?

Odong was offered a place at King's College Budo for his Higher School Certificate studies. He had never travelled beyond Lira- his home town. How would he get to Budo?

His grandfather told him of his travels during World War II. In 1943 Okelo, a recruit in the army, travelled to Soroti, Tororo, Jinja, and Kampala. One of his officers had been a teacher at Budo. Budo was not far from Kampala in the south of Uganda.

Later that night Okelo assured his grandson that getting to Budo was easy. "Many roads have been built since the War. It is no longer necessary to pass through Tororo and Jinja. The shorter route is through Kigumba and Luwero. A Budo school bus collects pupils from the central bus park in Kampala".

Why did Odong want to go to a school so far away from home? He wanted to be an electronics engineer. His head teacher had told him that the best physics teaching in the country was at Budo. There was a good library too.

Odong's mind was focused on his dream. He worked hard at school. His parents encouraged and helped him to prepare for his exams.

Many professions (law, medicine, engineering, nursing, etc.) require many years of basic training and apprenticeship before qualifying to

11

practice. The student must study set subjects and pass approved examinations to meet entry requirements. She must be willing and able to continue with her studies while former classmates are in employment and earning money.

1.3 Working at your goals

It is not enough to set goals. You must work at achieving them. You need a strategy -plan. A personal goal is like a pregnancy. It is only when its is carried to term that its rewards can be held in your hands. Unconsummated goals are like miscarriages- unfinished dreams.

Let me tell you the story about two cousins, Turiyo and Kaino, who had dreams for academic advancement. Both had the brains.

Turiyo was his mother's favourite child. After P6, she persuaded him to train as a primary school teacher. However, he wanted to own a university degree. So after qualifying as a teacher, he enrolled onto a correspondence course with the Rapid Results College (RRC) to study for the School Certificate examinations.

Although he paid for the course, he did not study hard. He spent his free time in muramba bars. Often over a calabash of muramba or an occasional bottle of Bell beer he boasted of what he would do after getting his degree.

His 'muramba-friends' laughed at him for "wasting money on book knowledge".
"What are you reading for: a headache? Leave books to your children" His uncle, a P2 dropout, would torment him.
"Look at yourself. A big school master. Why waste money on books? Behave like a man." An alcoholic neighbour advised.

On those few occasions when Turiyo stayed home studying, his drink-mates had less muramba than usual. It was in their interests to keep him away from books.

INTRODUCTION

Turiyo spent fewer and fewer evenings and weekends studying. Eventually he gave up. He continued to boast about his cleverness and how he wanted to study for a university degree but had no time.

His cousin, Kaino, also a primary school teacher, enrolled with the RRC a few months after Turiyo. He had been impressed by the RRC booklets. The college taught most O-level examination courses. He enrolled for Mathematics, History, Bible Knowledge, Geography, and English Language. The RRC could even prepare you for the HSC exams!

Kaino used every free moment to study. He was surprised to find that savings on alcohol more than covered the cost of the course. His drink-mates heaped scorn on him, but he persisted with his studies. He often wished that Turiyo would study seriously so that they could discuss difficult topics.

There were problems. Kaino's daughter was hospitalised with pneumonia three months before the exams. Though he had his booklets with him at the hospital, he could not concentrate on any subject. He was worried about her. Another month of school holidays, when he did most studying, was taken up by arrangements for his sister's wedding. But whenever he could he studied, and sent his assignments for correction and comment.

After 3 years of regular study, Kaino sat the O-level exam. He passed with credits in 4 of the 5 subjects he took. At about the same time he learnt that he could qualify for university study if he took and passed the mature entry exam. He passed the exam on the second attempt and was offered a place on a BA degree course.

Seven years after starting the RRC correspondence course, Kaino graduated from university with a BA degree. He had achieved his goal.

Turiyo occasionally mumbles about shortage of time to complete his correspondence course. He no longer boasts about his cleverness

2.3 Walk before you run
An ambitious young man wanted to open and run a shop. Was he willing to start humbly? No. Not Kapesa.

Nsimbi, Kapesa's uncle, is a friend of mine and a successful hotelier. Kapesa asked him for help in starting a business.
"What would you like to do?" Nsimbi asked his nephew.
"I do not know, Sir." Kapesa replied.
"Why don`t you open a small restaurant in your home town. On market days there are crowds of people and nowhere to buy food, or a drink. What do you think?" Nsimbi suggested.
"I have no transport, and no utensils."
"Your aunt could find you some pans, and I could lend you a bicycle. Find a suitable place and let me know soon "
"A bicycle is not enough, Sir."

Kapesa later complained to his friends that his uncle had refused to help him start a business.
"My uncle is a rich man. He should buy and stock a shop for me."
"Yeah man, he should", they mumbled; but secretly they laughed at his stupidity, and each wished he had a Nsimbi for an uncle.

A farmer prepares the land, sows the seed and weeds his fields before he expects a rich harvest. A baby crawls, walks hesitantly, often falling onto his bottom, before he can run.

- Have you decided on a particular career?
- Are you prepared to work hard at it until you succeed?
- Will you use every opportunity to prepare for your future?

INTRODUCTION

After secondary school, Kato decided to look for a job. He declined the degree course offered him at the local university. "It will take too long before I can earn money," he said. But he had more money than his friends! His father was a successful coffee grower. Kato had expensive tastes. He wanted more than his father would give him. He joined an insurance company as a salesman.

Several years later a former classmate, Mudusu, who had studied commerce at university joined the same company at a more senior level. Mudusu had a bigger salary, more responsibility and better opportunities.

Kato now wanted to go to university but he could not. He had acquired dependants (a wife and several children). He could not afford home study either. There were no local distance learning colleges and he could not afford foreign correspondence courses.

Your occupation must provide you with the basics for a normal life - *food, clothing, housing, health care*, and *personal fulfilment.* Humans also want jobs where they are considered useful by their neighbours. Jobs that make people feel important are in high demand. It is good to feel useful.

Summary

● Review your career, and plan your future. Study and practice until you are skilled. Become an expert.

● Will this career provide you with food, clothing, housing, health care, and vocational satisfaction?

● Say you can do it, you will do it, you have the ability, the spirit, and the stamina. Believe you can, and will succeed.

Only you know what you need/ want/ desire.

Further reading

A fuller discussion on motivation and goal setting may be found in the following books *[there are many more titles on the market]*.

1 *Turner, C.* **Born to Succeed**- How to Release Your Unlimited Potential. BCA 1994

2 *Carnegie, Dale.* **How to Win Friends and Influence People.** *Cedar 1981*

3 *Hill, Napoleon.* **Think and Grow Rich.** *Wilshire Books Co.1966*

4 *Waitley, Dennis.* **Empires of the Mind**-Lessons to lead and succeed in a knowledge-based world. *BCA 1995.*

5 *Covey, Steven R.* **The Seven Habits of Highly Effective People** -Restoring the character ethic. *Simon & Schuster 1992.*

6 *Robbins, Antony.* **Awaken the Giant within.** *Simon & Schuster 1992.*

2 Choosing a career

2 Choosing a career

2.1 Invest in yourself

How long would it take a 16 year old schoolgirl, or schoolboy to
become a graduate teacher, a surgeon, a nursing officer, a police
superintendent, an army captain, an air pilot, an accountant, or a
successful farmer? Years and many of them.

*A few months before taking the School Certificate examinations, we
had visits and talks from representatives of various occupations. In
1967 there were more jobs after O-levels exams than applicants.
Two Passes could get you a nice job or entry into a good training
institution.*

*Every speaker was convincing. Each was determined to recruit as
many people as possible. The training sounded easy, short and
enjoyable. Promotion would be certain and rapid. No problems.*

*After the policeman's speech Okelo saw himself in a police
inspector's uniform. After the soldier's talk I saw myself in a
general's uniform before my 30th birthday. After the doctor's
speech, Kizito saw himself as a brain surgeon in less than 10 years.
Migisha saw herself as chief nurse at a major hospital.*

At the time we did not appreciate how long it takes to advance in the
professions. Some require many years of training before
qualification. The following are examples (not including time spent
repeating courses and retaking examinations):

CHOOSING A CAREER

Profession	*Years after O-level (minimum) in Uganda*
teacher (BA/BSc)	5 years
lawyer (LLB)	5 years
midwife/ nurse (RM/RN)	3 years
veterinary officer (BVet M)	6 years
doctor (MB ChB)	7 years
surgeon (MMed Surg)	12 years

Whether to look for a job or continue with training for advanced qualifications depends on your circumstances.

• how badly do you need a job?
• how easy is it to find the right job, or any job?
• what are your qualifications, experience and skills?
• what are your dreams, goals, ambitions?

With the welcome increase in part time and correspondence (distance learning) courses, it is possible if you are determined, to continue with professional and general education and to hold a full time job at the same time.

2.2 Where to train?
Are you prepared to accept anything they offer you? Think twice before going to the interview, or enrolling onto the course:

• do you see your future in that profession?
• what qualifications will you get after the course?
• how tough is the competition for jobs in that occupation?
• will the training give you skills for self-employment?

New colleges and universities are opening in many towns. Many of these have excellent courses. However you should be selective in your choice of university and course. You should find out as much as possible about the college and the course before enrolling and parting with your money:

- does the college have enough qualified teachers?
- is it recognised by national licensing bodies?
- do employers readily recognise its diploma and degrees?
- are its qualifications recognised internationally?

2.3 How badly do you need a job?

If I were unemployed, and needed money to buy food, rent a room, or pay for the treatment of a sick relative, I would take any job that would help me pay for these. If you are employed, but want a more exciting job, you can afford to be choosy.

Similarly if you have somebody to support you (relative, friend, spouse, government) you can select a profession or job with better prospects even if the immediate rewards may be small.

Suppose you do not find a job. *Can you create one for yourself? Is there a service, or commodity you can provide, at a profit?* Look around, think! Many prosperous businesses started that way.

2.4 What are your qualifications?

If you wanted to be a doctor, a lawyer, an accountant but had only an O-level school certificate, you would have to obtain the required qualifications for university entrance. You might be able to study for some university degrees by correspondence, but it is easier if done at university. How long would it take? How would you pay for the course?

If I wanted to be a tailor, I would learn tailoring, then get a few years of experience working with an established tailor before setting up on my own.

Self taught people learn their trade on the job. The shopkeeper who started with nothing more than a box of assorted goods (soap, salt, sweets, matches, a bottle of aspirins, etc.) travelling from market to market is a typical example.

Rwomire started with a bicycle and a soapbox filled with matchboxes, pieces of soap, sweets, sugar, and other small items. He travelled to all markets in his gombolola (subcounty) selling his wares. His profit margins were small. His main meal was eaten at home with his wife and small children.

He saved every shilling he could. Gradually he acquired a larger box for his wares. He learnt to recognise the men and women who would pay their debts and those that would not. He learnt when to grant and when to refuse credit. Often he made mistakes and lost money. He learnt how to pick the goods that would sell. He learnt how to keep simple accounts and how to invest.

His savings multiplied and he built a shop on his shamba. His wife helped in the shop after her shamba work. They saved enough to build a permanent house, to eat better, and to send their children to school.

2.5 How ambitious are you?

Most normal people have ambitions. It is the size of their ambitions that differ. We want to eat well, to dress nicely, and to live in comfortable houses. We crave respect from our neighbours.

You should divide the process of achieving your ambitions into smaller tasks. Work at these tasks one at a time. When all the tasks are successfully completed, you will have achieved your goal. Through small incremental steps an exciting career is built. A baby must crawl, and learn to walk before running in the Olympics.

2.6 Beware of dead-end jobs

If you want steady promotions and recognition for your work you should be careful in your choice of employment. While most civil service jobs have structures for promotion, there are some departments with very little or no opportunity for promotions however good your service.

The police, teaching, the army, nursing, and the civil services are examples of professions with opportunities for advancement within their structure.

Occupations with limited opportunities for advancement include game ranger, medical assistant, dispensing, and many others in the health care and service industries. They have restricted (if any) options for promotions within the service, however good and ambitious you may be. One could use these jobs to earn a living while studying privately for more rewarding occupations.

Think twice before taking a dead-end job or training. You may never get out. Often it is wise to accept a job with a smaller salary but with opportunities for advancement, for learning skills that will lead to better things, or enable you to become self employed.

2.7 Self employment?

Many intelligent youths take up government jobs, not because they are fired with the spirit of public service, but because they do not want to get their hands dirty. Are you one of them? For a hard self employment than in public sector jobs.

It is sad to hear intelligent people say that manual jobs are for the less educated. Many self employed parents think that after getting an education, their son or daughter will run the family business. *"With his learning he will make my business more successful".* But unfortunately the boy is work-shy. He is too lazy and too proud to work with his hands.

What is he proud of when he cannot even equal the achievements of his less educated parents? They fed and clothed him and sent him to school. Can he do the same for his children?

You want a desk job, don't you?
Who will be your boss?
- the owner of your favourite restaurant -wasn't he once a *mandazi* boy?
- the owner of the lady's fashion shop -wasn't she once a seamstress?
- and the furniture shop where your cousin works -wasn't the owner a timber boy? Yes?

Learn a trade (motor mechanics, photography, carpentry, catering dressmaking, farming, etc.) Find a job, or take a course where you can learn a skill that may enable you to become your own boss in future. *But do you want to be self employed?*

Be optimistic. You may even become the boss --in future!

Abdu went to work in his uncle's garage in Natete at 17 years of age. His former classmates thought he was stupid. He had done well at school. He had several good O-level passes and could have secured an HSC place at a good school.

He began as a handy boy helping whichever mechanic needed a hand. His uncle bought him a book on motor mechanics. He read the book and watched senior mechanics at work. He observed, listened and followed instructions. He learnt from the experts. Within a few years he was a competent mechanic.

Today (many years later) former classmates beg him to accept their cars into his garage for repair. As garage manager, Abdu employs many mechanics. He supervises and manages the garage. He is planning and saving to open his own garage in another part of the city.

You should not restrict your thinking to government jobs, or jobs in large companies. Jobs in public enterprises and the civil service are getting more and more scarce every year. There are some unemployed university graduates walking the streets. You don`t have to join them.

If you find a non-government job with good prospects don`t let it slip through your fingers. All big companies were once small.

Recently I have had the feeling that some young people are in such a hurry to earn money that they are unwilling to learn new skills, take a course, or even wait for applications to be processed, to ensure more rewarding careers.

Katebe is a typical example. He passed his HSC examinations well and was accepted for a B.Com. degree course at Makerere University in Kampala. Instead he joined a new Forex bureau as a clerk. He would study commerce by correspondence, he told his parents. But life was too enjoyable for him to do much night studying. He did not go beyond enrolling for the course

A few year later the bureau was closed for improper trading. Katebe had no job, no qualification. No bank or Forex bureau wanted him.

2.8 Asking for help

Before asking for help, work out in detail what it is you want.
Remember Kapesa, the young man who asked his uncle for help in
starting a business? Had he thought out his objectives and set a clear
plan, his uncle would have helped him. *Before asking for help -*
Think:

- what do you want to do ?
- do you really need help?
- how much can you do on your own?
- how much have you done on your own?
- what would you do if you had the means?
- can you start on a smaller scale --one step at a time?
- do you really want to do that, or are you just imitating others?

2.9 A job is not life

A job, an income (money) lubricates life, but is not life. Dedicate
time and space for other interests, for family, for hobbies.

Many fathers spend so much time earning a living that they hardly
know their children, and drift away from their spouses. They have no
time to develop shared interests with the children; nor to maintain
them with spouses.

Examine your current position; where do you stand?

- Suppose you lost this job, have you skills for another career?
- Do you have friends away from your work?
- Have you kept affectionate contact with friends, and family.
- Are you saving and investing (money and time) in acquiring
  skills) for hard times, for retirement?
- How will you spend your time when you retire?
etc.

Further Reading

1 *Turner, C.* **Born to Succeed**- How to Release Your Unlimited Potential. *BCA 1994*

2 *Carnegie, Dale.* **How to Win Friends and Influence People.** *Cedar 1981*

3 *Hill, Napoleon.* **Think and Grow Rich.** *Wilshire Books Co.1966*

4 *Waitley, Dennis.* **Empires of the Mind**-Lessons to lead and succeed in a knowledge-based world. *BCA 1995.*

5 *Covey, Steven R.* **The Seven Habits of Highly Effective People** -Restoring the character ethic. *Simon & Schuster 1992.*

3 Writing Letters

3 Writing Letters

3.1 Why write?

Writing letters will increasingly become more important in your occupational and private life. So learn how to write letters that do their job well.

My letters are usually brief and factual. I write to keep in touch with friends and relatives, for business and professional purposes. My letters have objectives, [aims, important functions].

Your letter should say what you want it to say; no more, no less.
o think of what you are going to say and how you will say it.
o write politely; there is no need to record your rudeness.
o avoid ambiguity; your message should be clearly understood.
o use clear simple words, avoid jargon wherever possible.
o use short words, short sentences, and short paragraphs.
o avoid superfluous words and phrases *[gobbledegook]*.

3.2. Do you have to write it?

Letters are often kept by individuals and almost always by organisations, and are read again. Do you want the contents of your letter on permanent record? When dealing with large organisations it is usually best to put your considered case in writing. However you must think carefully before writing things down. Write, read, and rewrite your letter till it says what you want to say -no more no less. You will not be able to retract and amend it after it is dispatched.

A letter may be used as evidence in case of disagreement. It may support your case or may be used against you.

Do you need to write this letter?
Have you talked to the intended recipient? Can you get what you want without writing the letter? If you have to write (and often you must), then do it well.

3.3 Structure of a letter
A letter has a structure, (and each of its parts has a function):

* writer's address
* the date
* the addressee's name and address
* the greeting
* the message
* the closing phrase
* writer's signature and printed name.

3.3.1 The writer's address [with postcodes]
This is where the reply should be sent --a post office box number and location -*[World Bank, PO Box 7157, Kampala, Uganda];* or premises (private or public) -*[60 St. Fabians Drive, Chelmsford CM1 2PR].*

The method of delivering mail (letters, parcels, etc.) determines the form of address and postcodes. E.g:

* 60 St. Fabians Drive, Chelmsford CM1 2PR.
  (mail delivered to the house).

* Bank of Uganda, PO Box 7120, Kampala, Uganda.
  (mail placed in numbered box at post a office).

Postcodes and Zip codes are combinations of letters and digits used as part of a postal address to aid the sorting and delivery of mail:

- *Beihireyo Books, 60 St Fabians Drive, Chelmsford*
  CM1 2PR, England.

- *William & Wilkins, 428 East Preston Street, Baltimore*
  MD 21202 USA

CM1 2PR is the style of a post codes in Britain and, *MD 21202* is the style in the USA *(where it is called a zip code).*

House number
Many addresses have numbers identifying the building or plot on a street (avenue, boulevard, crescent, drive, lane, road, way, etc.).

60 St. Fabians Drive = House Number 60 on St. Fabians Drive. The number should be included in the address. While famous people and institutions can be found without the full address, mail for ordinary individuals may not be delivered if the full address is not given.

If you do not provide an address then you will not get a reply, unless the addressee already knows you and your address.

3.3.2 The date of writing
This fixes the letter in history -when was this letter written?
The date is particularly important in business and legal transactions.
- When was the order made, despatched, and paid for?
- When was the promise (or contract) made?

3.3.3 References
References (**Your Ref.../Our Ref...**) are vital in business and official letters. They relate the letter to previous communications (what has been written, ordered, agreed, refused, or postponed, *before*).

An official letter may also contain the initials of the officer who initiated, and the secretary who typed it -E.g: DT/MB.

Business letters also quote *Order No*..... and/or *Invoice No*...... when referring to orders and invoices for the purchase or sale of goods. These numbers are needed in the handling, despatching, and payment for, the goods. Their use speeds up business transactions. Quote them in your business letters as appropriate.

3.3.4 The addressee's (receiver's) name
The name of the addressee *[individual or officer to whom the letter is directed -the receiver],* should be written. This ensures that the letter goes straight to the right person or officer, and speeds up business and official communications.

3.3.5 The receiver's address
The residential or postal address to which the letter is sent should also be written, particularly in business and official letters. E.g:

Mr E Ntomi   *The Manager*
60 St. Fabians Drive   *Uganda Crafts*
Chelmsford   *PO Box 7047*
Essex CM1 2PR   *Kampala.*

Did I hear you say that you will write the address on the envelope? Envelopes are normally thrown away after removing the letter. So include the addressee's name and address on the letter too.

Personal letters often omit this item. It is better to include it unless you are writing to close friends and relatives. If you are not sure include the addressee's name and address.

3.3.6 The greeting
A greeting is used to start a letter: to greet the receiver. It is pure and simple politeness, like saying *Good morning* to somebody when you

don't care whether his morning is good or terrible.

Dear Sir, Dear Madam; Dear Mr Mume; Dear Mrs Muke, Dear Miss Muhara are typical phrases used to start letters. The word *Dear* does not mean the addressee is a loved friend or relative. Letters to enemies also start with *Dear*....

3.3.7 The message

This is the reason for writing. If you want somebody to understand and act on the basis of your letter, then give him or her the full picture. Write clearly and concisely giving the facts and details so that the reader gets the *message.*

So before you put pen to paper *[or touch the keyboard], think.*
- What do you want to say?
- How do you want to say it (tone)?
- What will you exclude from this letter?
- What would you want to know if you were the recipient?

3.3.8 Re: .... Subject: ....

Business and official letters frequently have headings to the body of the letter. This states the subject of the letter. Headings may start with **Re:** (in the matter of) or with **Subject:**

Re: *Application for post of personnel director*
Subject: *Request for study leave, 15 -30 January.*

In the past the subject of the letter was usually underlined. e.g: Re: <u>Request for study leave 15-30 January</u>.

The fashion now is to type it in bold letters (highlighting). e.g:
Re: **Absenteeism Among Factory workers.**

3.3.9 The closing phrase (signing off)

Ending a letter is similar to starting it. A friendly phrase is used. In business, and official letters the closing phrase is usually one of the following:

Yours sincerely (if the letter started with a personal name)
Yours faithfully (if official titles only have been used)
Your obedient servant (by a junior official to a senior)

These phrases have nothing to do with sincerity, faithfulness (trust) obedience, or servitude. They are mere customs [historical remnants of English politeness] used to end letters -no more and no less. Polite letter writers use them. The first two are more frequently used than the third. You may also use them until you invent something better.

Phrases that end letters to relatives and close friends include:
Your affectionate (daughter, son, ..)
Yours affectionately
With love
Your (niece, ..)
Yours

Keep these for letters to close friends and relatives. They are impolite when used in official communications or in letters to strangers.

3.3.10 Writer's signature and name

The writer's signature and printed name should follow the closing phrase. Do you want your letter answered? Make it easy - print your name below your signature:

Yours sincerely

E S Muhogo

Mr E S Muhogo

Official title/ or position
In business and official letters, it is useful to indicate the writer's position in the organisation. E.g:

EMJoughrod

Eric M.Toughrod
Associate Collector, Samson Debt-Call Ltd

Titles are helpful to new members and recruits (particularly in large organisations). They relate individuals' names to official positions and functions, and facilitate communication.

They are also helpful in subsequent telephone communications when somebody may ask -*What does she/he do here?*

3.4 Examples of common letters

3.4.1 'Thank you' Letters
A *'Thank you'* letter is written to thank somebody for a service or favour received. It is usually brief and to the point.

Mrs Nkombe was unable to take her son Peter to Kitante Primary School entrance interview. A friend, Mrs Mary Ogwang took the child. Mrs Nkombe wrote the following note to say 'Thank you' to Mary.

Mrs Nkombe starts her letter with *Dear Mary* because they are close friends. She only needs to sign her name. Mrs Ogwang knows Joyce Nkombe`s signature.

University Library
PO Box 7062,
Kampala

12 September 1995

Dear Mary

Thank you so much for taking Peter to the Kitante interview; and for giving him lunch. He enjoyed going with you. He says he answered all the questions to please Mum`s friend.

I got a letter from the school today. Peter has been offered a place for next January.

Thanks.

Joyce Nkombe

3.4.2 Applying for a work experience attachment

Kirk R Krypton, a 16 year old school boy seeks placement for work experience. He is interested in computers and wrote to computer companies including Herzian Computers of Harlow.

45 Argon Avenue
Blackmore, Essex

23 April 1995

Mr Peter Herz
The Manager
Herzian Computers
56 Helios Drive.
Harlow CM20.

Dear Mr Herz,

Re: Request for a work experience attachment

Would you allow me to spend 4 weeks at Herzian Computers in August 1995 for my work experience.

I am a 16 year old pupil at Rochefort School, in Blackmore. As part of my education I am required to spend some time in a workplace to experience the routine and discipline of work.

I am interested in computers and use one for my homework. I am learning programming in C+.

During my stay at Herzian Computers I hope to learn about selling computers and serving customers.

Thank you for your help

Yours sincerely

XXrypton

Kirk Krypton

3.4.3 Applying for a job
After formal education your professional progress will depend on your skills in securing jobs, courses, and services *(Chapters 5 & 6)*.

J. Namukasa applied for the post of personal secretary. This is the letter that accompanied her CV:

Matoke Corporation
PO Box 888x, Kampala

15 June 1994

The Personnel Officer
Dairy Corporation
PO Box 7078, Kampala.

Dear Sir

Re: Personal secretary to the corporation director

The post of personal secretary to the director is important to the corporation's work.

My skills will enable me to fill it competently and efficiently:
● a diploma in secretarial studies,
● fluency in French and Kiswahili,
● skills in using computers in for business communication.

I am enclosing a detailed curriculum vitae, and look forward to hearing from you.

Yours faithfully,

Jane Namukasa
JANE NAMUKASA

3.4.4 Accepting Invitation (for Interview)

Alice Awino has been invited for interview for the post of School Inspector (biology teaching) in the Ministry of Education. She is writing to say she will attend the interview.

Bombo High School
PO Box 777x
Bombo.

20 October 1994

Mr S Mfundishi
Chief School Inspector
Ministry of Education,
PO Box 7063
Kampala.

Dear Mr Mfundishi

Re: Interview for School Inspector (Biology teaching)

Thank you for inviting me for interview on the 9th November 1994 for the post of School Inspector (biology teaching).

I will attend the interview, and as requested, will bring my certificates and copies of my publications.

Yours sincerely,

Alice Awino

ALICE AWINO

3.4.5 Letter of Resignation

*John Magezi has been admitted to a college in the USA. He now
writes to the Town Clerk to resign from his job.*

Town Clerk`s Office
Kabale

20 May 1994

The Town Clerk
Kabale.

Dear Sir

Subject: Resignation from the post of Clerical Officer

I have enjoyed working in your department since I joined it
in 1981. Thank you for giving me the opportunity to be of
service to my community, and for earning a living.

As you already know, I have been offered a scholarship to
study theology and church management in the USA starting
next September.

Please accept my resignation as of 31 August 1994.

May I take the remainder of my annual leave (25 days) from 6
August 1994.

Your obedient servant

John Magezi

JOHN MAGEZI

3.4.6 Letters of Inquiry

In a letter of inquiry you request for information about some service, activity or merchandise. Your letter should state all the questions you want answered.

Buying a Japanese Van
Mark Gweno does not know how to buy a reconditioned van from Japan. He writes asking how he might order the van.

Gweno Transport Ltd,
P O Apach, Uganda.

17 May 1991

Yutaka Co ltd,
3-5-13 Ohsu, Naku-ku,
Nagoya, Japan.

Dear Sirs

Re: Purchase of a Toyota or Nissan passenger van.

I would like to buy a reconditioned 1988-1990 Toyota or Nissan (20-24 seater) passenger van from your company.
1 How much will it cost -by models, age, and size?
2 How do I pay for the van - currency, and method?
3 How will the van reach me? Do you have agents in Uganda?
4 How long does the warranty last (workmanship and parts)?

Yours faithfully,

Mark Gweno

MARK GWENO

3.4.7 Ordering for goods

When you order goods by letter you must ensure that your instructions are clear, and simple. State the exact make of goods, the quantities you want, and details about packing and dispatch as necessary. If the prices have been previously agreed then remind the supplier in your order.

Ordering a book

Book orders should give enough information so that the exact book you want can be identified. Books are identified by title (name of the book), author or editor, edition (version of the book) year of publication, and publisher (company or individual who paid for producing the book).

All these details are needed because:

- there are many books with identical titles, but different contents;
- books with identical titles may have different publishers;
- often there are different versions (editions) of the same book;
- authors with similar names may have written books on the same subject; etc.

Ordering merchandise
Mr Ahmed Kitara, a trader from Masindi ordered trade goods.

A M Kitara Stores Ltd,
PO Box 66x, Masindi

15 March 1993

Mr Abdulla Kamali
Kamali Merchants Ltd,
Wandegeya, Kampala.

Dear Abdulla,

Re: Order of goods -Mr M Bifandimu will collect them

Thank you for sending the items I ordered last January. They arrived safely in the right quantities.

Please send me the following on the terms recently agreed:
4 rolls of Nytil light green Kaki cloth -(for boys' shorts)
5 rolls of Nytil white cloth -(for boys' shirts)
20 kilograms of assorted hard sweets.
50 dozen HB pencils -(the type made in Jinja)
100 dozen Karoli 24 page school exercise books

Mr M Bifandimu will collect and bring the goods in his van.

May Allah bless your business.

Yours sincerely,

AMKitara

AHMED M KITARA

Ruth Kalaamu wants to learn how to write novels. Recently she saw a book with an enticing title - "Writing the Novel -from plot to print", with one of her lecturers. She orders for a copy through a local bookshop.

Africa Hall`
PO Box 16320
Kampala

9 March 1994

The Manager
St Paul`s Book Centre
Kampala.

Dear Madam

**Re: Book Order - "Writing the Novel -from plot to print"
by L. Block**

Would you obtain for me a copy of **'Writing the Novel -from plot to print'** by L Block. It is published by Writer`s Digest Books, 1979. (Writers Digest Books, 9933 Alliance Road, Cincinnati Ohio 45242, USA.)

Let me know if you require a deposit before placing the order.

Yours faithfully

R.S.Kalaamu

Ruth S Kalaamu

3.4.8 Letters of complaint

If your complaint is aimed at getting your problem solved, your letter should clearly state the problem and the help your request.

Anne's brother sent her a registered parcel. She has not received it

---

Nkumba College of Commerce
PO Box 237, Entebbe.

23 April 1995

The Postmaster
PO Box 7171, Kampala.

Dear Sir

Re: Missing Registered Airmail Parcel

A registered airmail parcel was posted to me from London, U.K. in January 1995. I have not received it yet.
Posted at The post office, Euston, London, WC2.
Sender: Mr P.Musomo; 30 Guilford Street, London WC2.
Addressee: Miss Anne Musomo; Nkumba College of Commerce, PO Box 237, Entebbe, Uganda.
Registration No: R 0012345 ; Posted 16 January,1995.
Content: A book - *Winning At Your Interviews* by M. Stevens
Value : £ 9.00 (about USh 13000/=)

I will be grateful for your assistance in tracing the parcel.

Yours faithfully,

Anne Musomo

ANNE MUSOMO

A letter of complaint should state its purpose clearly.
o Why are you writing the letter?
o What should the recipient do after reading your letter?

Do you want:
o compensation for lost property or missed service?
o a refund for spoilt or lost goods?
o help to solve the problem?

Blowing off steam

Mr Ngendo Msafiri was disappointed with the services at Sleeper's Paradise. He writes to tell the manager about his experience.

                                        Sleeper's Paradise
                                          Kampala.

6 August 1995

Mr Samson Ndeire
Manager, Sleeper's Paradise.

Dear Mr Ndeire

Subject: Poor Service in Your Lodge -Lost Customer?
In the past, Sleeper's Paradise was a traveller's joy. Two days ago I booked into your lodge expecting the usual high standard of service. I was disappointed.

The bed sheets were less than clean. The curtains could not keep out the street light. The service was so slow that I had to abandon several meals otherwise I would have missed my business appointments.

I am writing to say that I did not have two nights in paradise. Do you still recommend Sleeper's Paradise to your friends?

Your disappointed customer.
Ngendo Msafiri
NGENDO MSAFIRI

3.4.9 Lobbying your MP
Mr S. Mugisha regularly drives to Rukungiri via Kambuga. The road is rough and frequently impassable. He wants his MP to lobby for its repair. He tells his MP about the road -as if the MP did not use the same route to Kampala.

Kihihi Chamber of Commerce
PO Kihihi, Rukungiri,

21 November 1994

The Honourable MP for Kihihi
National Assembly
PO Box 7178, Kampala.

Honourable Sir,

Re: Repairs to the Kihihi-Kambuga-Rukungiri Road

Thank you for being our hard working MP. We are lucky to have you as our representative in the National Assembly. We follow you performance in the house with interest.

Honourable Sir, we would like to remind you of the state of the Kihihi-Kambuga-Rukungiri road.

I drive on this road at least once a week. My pickup has been shaken into pieces by the boulders and holes that make the road surface. Most of my income is spent on repairs -tyres, suspensions, etc.

....../2

2

Your elderly constituents are not too happy either. There are
no buses on this road! Their rheumatism is not helped by pickup
journeys to Kambuga or worse to Rukungiri. They are afraid
of travelling by pickup to Kambuga or Nyakibare Hospitals.
The journey may be more dangerous than their ailments.

We, members of the Kihihi Chamber of Commerce and your
constituents, know that your are a hard working MP. We
know that Kambuga Hospital has been rehabilitated and we
appreciated your efforts.

Would you now use your influence and skill again to get the
Kihihi-Kambuga-Rukungiri road repaired.

Sure, we would appreciate a tarmac surface.

Thank you again for being our MP.

Yours sincerely

SMugisha

SULEIMAN MUGISHA
Secretary, Kihihi Chamber of Commerce.

Further Reading

Venolia, Jan. **Write Right** -a Desk Drawer Digest of Punctuation,
Grammar and Style. *David & Charles 1986.*

4 *Write Your Curriculum Vitae*

4 Write Your Curriculum Vitae

4.1 What is a curriculum vitae?
Your curriculum vitae (CV) is a written summary of your life and work- [personal details, education, qualifications, skills, work]. It also includes your hobbies and other interests. CVs are also called *Career Summary* or *Biodata*.

4.2 What is a CV for?
The purpose of a CV is to secure you an interview [with the employer you want to work with, the college you wish to enrol at, the bank you seek a loan from, the grants committee, etc]. A well prepared CV is an asset in the competition for scarce educational or occupational opportunities. It should be **clear, concise, precise,** and **simple.**

You can use your CV:
- when applying for advertised jobs
- when applying for training positions
- when applying for a bank loan
- as an introduction to institutions (college, company, etc).

4.3 Structure of a CV
CVs are as different as the individuals they describe. Nevertheless they all cover essential items -Personal details, Qualification(s) Education, Employment, Interests/Hobbies, Referees.

The following is a frequently used format.

NAME
ADDRESS

TELEPHONE NUMBER
FACSIMILE NUMBER

DATE OF BIRTH
NATIONALITY
MARITAL STATUS

EDUCATION
Dates   *Name and location of school or college*
             Subjects studied and qualifications
             Outstanding non-academic achievements

QUALIFICATIONS

SKILLS AND EXPERIENCE
   List of your main skills and abilities

EMPLOYMENT
Dates   *Employer's name and address*
             Position held, and main duties

INTERESTS (HOBBIES)

ADDITIONAL INFORMATION
Useful facts that do not fit well into the above categories
(Omit this if you have no additional information to give)

REFERENCES
Names, addresses, telephone numbers of your referees

An alternative format

NAME
ADDRESS

TELEPHONE NUMBER

CAREER STATEMENT

CAREER AND ACHIEVEMENTS TO DATE
(In reverse chronological order)

PROFESSIONAL QUALIFICATIONS AND TRAINING
(Starting with highest qualification, and highest educational level)

HOBBIES AND INTERESTS

PERSONAL DETAILS
(Date of birth, nationality, marital status)

The second format may be better for recruiters in business. It gives the information in the order it is normally used to make the decision on whether to call for interview or to reject.

4.3.1 Personal details -your names, address, telephone number (where available), date of birth, nationality, marital status, etc. *[Students may need to give holiday and term time addresses].*

4.3.2 Education -give the dates, names and addresses of schools and colleges and universities you attended; and details of courses taken and examinations passed.

4.3.3 Qualifications -state the qualifications you hold: e.g: GCSE, BA, RN, LLB, MBA, Certificate in Catering, etc.; and *membership (by examination) of professional bodies (ACCA, FRCS, MICE...).*

4.3.4 Employment -give dates, names of employers and their addresses; job titles, and your duties and responsibilities. Clearly state your achievements in each position. You future employer is interested in your skills *(what you know, and what you can do and have done)*; and not empty *years of experience*.

4.3.5 Publications
If you have published papers, articles or books then include them in your CV. Cite your publications, giving names of author(s), title of the paper or book, the journal (name, date, volume, and pages) or publisher and dates. E.g:

1 Turya, EB. Medical Assistant in Uganda: a profile. *World Health Forum* 1984, 5(3): 231-232.
   [5(3): 231-232 means Volume 5, Number 3, pages 231-232].

2 Turya, EB. *Write them Right*. Beihireyo Books 1996
   ISBN 0-9515819-5-3.

Often an ISBN *(International Standard Book Number)* is quoted. *0-9515819-5-3* is the ISBN for this edition of *Write them Right*. It identifies the publisher, and the book (title). ISBNs help bookshops, libraries and individuals to trace and order books.

4.3.6 Hobbies/ Interests

The purpose of this section is to show that you have a life outside your work. Name and briefly describe your hobbies, and leisure activities. If you are captain of a competitive team say so. Your role in community activities, charity groups; your church, mosque or synagogue may be described here.

Do not include activities likely to offend prospective employers. Be sensitive in choice of words.

4.3.7 Additional Information includes any other information you wish the recruiter to know, but could not fit into the other sections of the CV:

- career plans (jobs you seek, or training you plan to take)
- relevant courses and seminars you have attended recently
- general and professional courses you are engaged in now
- special abilities (leadership, team building, etc.)
- special professional, or linguistic skills.

4.3.8 Referees are people who know you well (from work, school/ college/ university) and are able and willing to commend you to a new employer or other organisations. Give the names, addresses, telephone numbers of 2 or 3 persons who have *agreed* to give references on your character, and skills.

Use people who will put in a good word for you. *If you suspect that somebody will give you a bad reference do not use his or her name!*

While academic and public service organisations usually want names of referees on your CV, business recruiters (for senior positions) ask for referees only from promising prospects. You could omit referees from CVs aimed at business and industry. But be ready to provide the names promptly.

4.4 Types of CV

A CV can be prepared in three slightly different ways: Chronological, Functional, or Targeted.

4.4.1 *A Chronological CV* lists work experience from the first job to the last (most recent). This is suitable for candidates who want to stay in the same industry or profession, and who have a relative short work record or have not changed jobs frequently.

4.4.2 *A Functional CV* lists professional qualifications, and highlights functional competencies (skills and expertise). Work experience is summarised.

4.4.3 *A Targeted CV* is suitable for young candidates looking for their first substantive post. It names the targeted job (what he/she is aiming for). It states the candidate's capabilities (skills) and:
- Lists accomplishments in school or college and qualifications;
- Gives her work experience (while at school or college);
- Lists hobbies and other interests and;
- Gives names of referees.

4.4 Preparing your CV

Many people are reluctant to write their CV, fearing that they will get it wrong. The more you practice at writing your CV the better it will become.

To prepare your CV get a large sheet of paper and [*following the CV formats on p51,52*] write down all the information you can about yourself. If you have just finished school or college you will not have much to write under *employment* and *publications*. You should have more to write under *hobbies*.

WRITE YOUR CURRICULUM VITAE

Let us help a fictitious young man, John Magezi, write his CV:

John attended Kigezi College where he played on the school football team, and was president of the debating society. He was a school prefect in his final school year. He passed 5 subjects at the O-level School Certificate examinations.

Since leaving school he has been working as a clerical officer in Kabale Town Clerk's office. He sings in the church choir and is active in church activities. He regularly plays football. Last year he married Ruth a long term sweetheart and they recently had a baby boy (Michael).

His church has selected him to study theology and management at a college in the USA. An American church will pay for his studies. Magezi needs a place at an American college.

He is excited about going to America; but he has never applied for a university place in his life. **What should he do ?**

Let me show you how to prepare a *chronological* CV for John from his personal, educational and employment history and hobbies. The result should make the Americans happy to give him a place in their college. I will be concise, but informative *(page 57)*.

4.6 What to exclude from the CV
Your CV should present you in the best light. On its strength you will either be selected for further consideration or rejected. Often places on courses; and occasionally jobs; are given on the strength of CVs only. It has happened to me several times.

Therefore your CV should be *concise, precise and simple.* It should contain no false claims. Lies may be exposed through your referees, at interview or later, then you would be dismissed.

NAME	**John MAGEZI**
ADDRESS	Town Clerk's office,
	PO Kabale, Uganda

DATE OF BIRTH	9th October 1966, Kabale, Uganda
NATIONALITY	Ugandan
MARITAL STATUS	Married with 1 child .

EDUCATION

1973-1979 Kabale Primary School, Kabale.
1980-1983 Kigezi College, Butobele, Kabale (a high school).

Subjects Passed at School Certificate Exam, 1983

English	4	Bible Knowledge	3
Geography	5	History	4
Mathematics	4		

Notable achievements at high school were:
- captained the school football (soccer) team (1982-83)
- school prefect; president of the debating society (1983).

EMPLOYMENT

1984-1985: **clerical assistant,** Town Clerk's office, Kabale:
- sorted and forwarded mail to various offices
- drafted replies for the deputy town clerk`s correspondence.

1986 -to date: **Clerical officer,** Town Clerk's office, Kabale:
- clerk-in-charge of environmental health issues,
- administrative assistant to the environmental health director
- supervising and training clerical assistants.

2

HOBBIES
- Playing soccer,(captained Town Clerk`s team 1991-93).
- Singing in parish church choir,
- Member of the parish social welfare group
  - we organise prayer meetings at the church and in homes
  - we raise funds for the welfare of orphans in the township.

REFEREES

Rev. Peter Owangye	Mr Thomas Barebehe
Bugongi Parish	Kabale Town Clerk
PO Kabale, Uganda.	PO Kabale, Uganda.

You will not be appointed if, at the interview you show no evidence of the knowledge and skills your CV claims you have. Your CV should contain verifiable statements only.

However it is not necessary to present yourself in a negative way. You should emphasise your positive achievements. John Magezi did not record that he failed Physics, Chemistry, and Agriculture. He recorded his modest passes in English, Geography, Mathematics History, and Bible Knowledge. His skills in football, debating, and singing were highlighted. Public speech and singing are useful skills for church leaders.

Prospective employers are more interested in your successes -what you can do. So emphasise your strong points: your *potential for success.*

In Chapter 6, *(Taking Interviews)*, I shall discuss how to openly talk about your past failures and errors (the lessons learnt from them!).

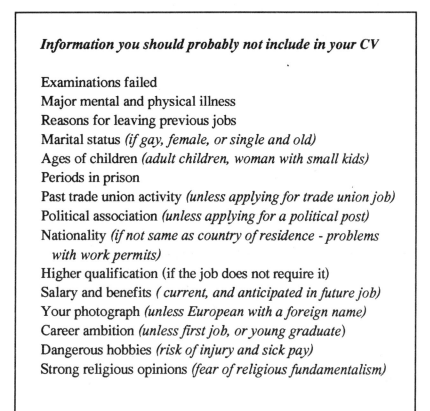

Information you should probably not include in your CV

Examinations failed
Major mental and physical illness
Reasons for leaving previous jobs
Marital status *(if gay, female, or single and old)*
Ages of children *(adult children, woman with small kids)*
Periods in prison
Past trade union activity *(unless applying for trade union job)*
Political association *(unless applying for a political post)*
Nationality *(if not same as country of residence - problems with work permits)*
Higher qualification (if the job does not require it)
Salary and benefits *(current, and anticipated in future job)*
Your photograph *(unless European with a foreign name)*
Career ambition *(unless first job, or young graduate)*
Dangerous hobbies *(risk of injury and sick pay)*
Strong religious opinions *(fear of religious fundamentalism)*

4.7 Length of CV

Academic institutions and professional bodies like detailed curricula vitae with every job and publications listed.

Business recruiters on the other hand want concise, action oriented CVs; (usually no more than 2 typed pages.

4.8 Quality of CV

The business employer wants candidates who demonstrate:

- flexibility (across tasks, products, national borders)
- speed of learning and adaptability to change
- organisation skills, leadership
- ability to motivate teams and task forces
- quality orientation, entrepreneurial success
- language skills (in addition to mother tongue)
- computer literacy.

4.9 Language of your CV

Your CV should be written in an active language. Emphasise your achievements, skills, contributions to success or profitability.

Use positive/action words wherever possible:

achieved,	established	productive
built	managed	supervised
co-ordinated	organised	trained
directed	participated	versatile etc.

4.10 Common errors in CV

The following are the errors commonly found in CVs:

- Too long, too fancy
- Misspelling and/or bad grammar
- Disorganised, too many irregularities
- Badly set out, poorly typed or copied
- Too many obvious omissions
- No mention of results.

4.11 Examples of curriculum vitae
[Let us read through a few Fictitious CVs].

1. Apuli Kajangu, a 19 year old school boy wants a job in sales. He names his target position.

NAME   **Apuli KAJANGU**

ADDRESS   c/o Bangonza Bookshop
                             PO Box 99x, Fort Portal.

DATE OF BIRTH   18 March 1975
NATIONALITY   Ugandan
SEX   Male
MARITAL STATUS Single

TARGET POSITION *Sales Assistant* (Trainee)

SKILLS AND POTENTIAL
I have the following skills:
● Leadership (I was soccer captain and school prefect).
● Communicating with customers (from current job, and fluency in English, Kiswahili and Rutoro).
● Salesmanship and Book keeping from my current job.

EDUCATION
1979-1985 **Kasese Primary School, Kasese**
1989-1994 **Nyakasura School, Fort Portal,**)
- played on the school football team; captain 1993-94
- effective house prefect, and school prefect (1994).
- 6 O-level passes (1992); 3 passes at A-level (1994) exams.

.../2

61

2

CURRENT EMPLOYMENT

January 1995: Shop Assistant, Bagonza Bookshop, Kabarole:
- setting up book displays and closing up in the evening
- serving customers (sales, orders, inquiries)
- assisting with book keeping and ordering new stock

HOBBIES
- Football; I am a member of Kabarole Panthers
  Listening to Music, and Dancing (popular and traditional).

ADDITIONAL INFORMATION
I am studying (GCE) Marketing and Accountancy by
correspondence with the Rapid Result College, London.
I believe that skills and qualifications in these subjects will
be useful in a future career in Sales and Marketing.

REFEREES

Mr Akiiki Bagonza   The Headteacher
Bagonza Bookshop   Nyakasura School
PO Box 99x, Fort Portal.   PO Box 16, Fort Portal

2. Jane Namukasa, a 23 years old secretary, looking for a new job

NAME   **Jane NAMUKASA**

ADDRESS   c/o Mr Semu Mukasa
                PO Box 44x Mukono.
                Telephone 234x6

DATE OF BIRTH   24 March 1970
NATIONALITY   Ugandan
MARITAL STATUS   Single

EDUCATION
1977 -1983 St Paul's Primary School, Mukono,
1984 -1987 St K Lwanga High School, Mukono.
- active in the school choir and the traditional dance troupe
- house prefect and captained the house netball team.

4 School Certificate Passes (1987)
      English 4   History   4
      Luganda 3   Agriculture 6

1988 -1990 Uganda College of Commerce, Kampala.
- Diploma in Secretarial Studies
- took extramural courses in French, and Computer skills

QUALIFICATIONS
Uganda School Certificate (O-level), 1987.
Diploma in Secretarial Studies, 1990
I am skilled in Computing for management and commerce.

..../2

2

EMPLOYMENT
1991 - to date: secretary to the Director, Matoke Corporation,
- general secretarial duties relating to the director's office;

HOBBIES
Listening to the radio for traditional and popular music.
Member of the Nakasero Traditional Music Club.
Making raffia mats, and handbags.

REFEREES
Mr Mohamad Ndizi
Director, Matoke Corporation,
PO Box 888x, Kampala.   Tel. 2345x7
                               Fax. 2728x9

Mrs Maria Kaziro,
Kawolo College of Commerce,
PO Box 77x, Kawolo.   Tel. 4455x6

3. Suleman Mugisha, a 25 year old farmer, seeks a bank loan

NAME   **Suleman MUGISHA**
ADDRESS   Kihihi Goat Farm
                    P O Kihihi, Rukungiri.

PURPOSE OF LOAN
My farming business needs the loan to invest in:
1 Refrigeration equipment for goat milk and meat
2 Building all-weather accommodation for farm animals.

MY EXPERIENCE IN FARMING
- I am skilled in the care of farm animals as business assets.
- I have enhanced my farm's productivity and profitability is 30% per year (over last 3 years).

EDUCATION
1977-1984: Kihihi Primary School (Passed P 7 Exam in 1984).
1990: attended a 6 months course small animal husbandry at Rukungiri Farm Institute. I passed the course assessments with commendation.

EMPLOYMENT
1985-1990: **Farmer trainee, Kihihi Goat Farm**
- cared for goats, and sheep, improved milk and meat yields
- acquired skills in coffee production
- maintained farm machinery with the farm mechanic

1991-1995 **Assistant farm manager**
- supervised employees in animal husbandry
- maintained (with an accounts clerk) the farm's accounts.
- managed the welfare of employees.

                                                          ..../2

2

ADDITIONAL INFORMATION

Audited accounts for the last three years are enclosed.
The farm is profitable with no debts or mortgages.

INTERESTS

Listening to the radio (politics, farming news, music).
Chairman of the Resistance Council (RC2).
Secretary Kihihi Chamber of Commerce.

DATE OF BIRTH	8 May 1970
NATIONALITY	Ugandan
MARITAL STATUS	Married with 4 children

Suleman would send this functional CV, the farm's Business Plan, a copy of the farm's audited accounts, and a covering letter to the bank manager. He would keep copies of these documents for his records, and for preparing for an interview with the banker.

Suleman's CV anticipates and answers important questions:
- Who is he (person, business)?
- Why does he want the money?
- Does he know his business?
- Will he be able to repay the loan (make money for the bank)?

4. James Kofi, a 34 year old expatriate doctor is applies for a post in cardiology in a British NHS hospital.

NAME   **James KOFI**
ADDRESS   Department of Medicine
                Bloomfield Hospital
                Essex CM1 5ET

DATE OF BIRTH   4 June 1961
NATIONALITY   Ghana
MARITAL STATUS Married with 2 children

QUALIFICATION
  MB ChB 1985 Accra University, Accra, Ghana
  MRCP   1994 Royal Colleges of Physicians (UK)

CAREER PLAN
I aim to gain practical skills in clinical cardiology before returning to Ghana to work in a mission hospital in Ashanti.

SKILLS AND EXPERIENCE
The skills I will bring to the departments include:
● Competent management of common cardiac disorders
● Efficient supervision of junior doctors and medical students
● Interest and competence in teaching medical students
● Experience and interest in clinical research and audit.

PROFESSIONAL ORGANISATIONS
  Full registration with the Ghana Medical Council
  Limited Registration with the General Medical Council
  Member of the Ghana Medical Association

.../2

2

EDUCATION
1967 -1979: Aurum School, Accra, Ghana
- Represented the school in basketball and athletics.
- 8 O-level passes (1977) and 3 A-level passes (1979)

1980-1985: Medical Studies, Accra Medical School
- Played on the university basketball (1982-84).
- Awarded MB CHB (with Distinctions in Medicine, Paediatrics and Public Health) in 1985.

EMPLOYMENT HISTORY
1985- 1986: House officer in Medicine and Surgery, St Luke's Hospital, Accra, Ghana

1987-1990: Senior House Officer in Cardiology, St Luke's Hospital, Accra, Ghana.

1991-1993: Senior House Officer in Geriatric Medicine, Leigh Infirmary, Leigh, Lancashire.

1994 -to-date: Visiting Registrar in Medicine Bloomfield Hospital, Essex

CLINICAL AUDIT
I audited, and presented at hospital audit meetings, the following subjects:

1 Ischaemic heart disease and income in adult males at St Luke's Hospital, Accra (1988-90).

2 Survival after myocardial infarction in females over 70 years of age treated at Leigh Infirmary (1992)

.../3

3

HOBBIES
Cycling and jogging;
Ghanaian and West African cooking.
History of Medicine

REFEREES

Dr Antony Habib	Dr. Michael Kwame
Leigh Infirmary	Bloomfield Hospital
Leigh WN7 1HS	Chelmsford CM1 5ET

5. Alice Awino, a 42 year old school teacher, seeks a senior post in the ministry of Education

NAME   Alice AWINO

ADDRESS   Bombo High School,
                    PO Box 77x, Bombo

DATE OF BIRTH   14th June 1953
NATIONALITY   Ugandan
MARITAL STATUS   Married with 6 children

QUALIFICATIONS
BSc Ed 1975 Makerere (Biology with Education)
MSc   1984 Makerere (Educational Psychology)

EDUCATION
1967 - 1972 **Tororo Secondary School, Tororo**
- national school athletics champion (200m, 400m)
- passed 7 O-levels in 1970; and 3 A-levels in1972.

1973-1975 **Makerere University, (BSc with Education)**
- a 3 year BSc (biological sciences and education) course
- university athletics team: 200m, 400m flat & relays (1973-74).

1983-1984 **Institute of Education, Makerere University**
- MSc in Educational Psychology, (course work, research)
- MSc awarded after written examination and an oral on the
  dissertation *[Home environment and scholastic attainment
  of children from urban slums].*

....l2

70

2

CURRENT EMPLOYMENT
1985 - to date: **Headteacher, Bombo High School, Bombo**
- school administration and supervising teacher trainees;
- senior biology teacher, health and hygiene instructor
- national examiner in school biology and health science.

PREVIOUS EMPLOYMENT
1976 -1983: **Biology teacher,** St K Lwanga School, Mukono
- house mistress, sports teacher for girls.
- national examiner in Biology and Health Science (1980).

PUBLICATIONS
1 Home environment and scholastic attainment of children
   from urban slums. An MSc dissertation, Institute of
   Educational, Makerere University, 1984

2 Home environment and scholastic attainment of children
   from urban slums. *National Teacher,* 1984; 6(8):23-25

3 **Basic Human Biology.** Vitabo Ltd, Kampala, 1989.

INTERESTS
Traditional Dancing; organise dance classes for students
Reading novels, and listening to music

REFEREES
Prof. Sam Wamali   Mr Ali Ndibota
Institute of Education   Ministry of Education
PO Box 7062   PO Box 7063
Kampala   Kampala

4.12 Every application - a new CV?

Yes. The CV should contain only information relevant to that particular application. No more, no less. It must address the recruiters needs. A general CV can not meet the requirements of every job/vacancy you may wish to pursue.

So do yourself a favour -send your best advocate:

- *write a fresh and focused CV for each application.*

- with word-processing a new CV can be produced from your computer fairly quickly; **otherwise:**

- keep several versions of your CV, select and send the most appropriate.

- if you use a general CV, ensure that the covering letter anticipates and answers the recruiters needs (questions).

- update your CV frequently, and keep the copies clean.

CVs are used to select (short list) candidates before interviews. Your CV speaks and pleads for you. Prepare and send your best delegate.

I have had job offers on the strength of my CV only. Many capable applicants have missed good positions because their CVs were tattered, untidy, or plainly irrelevant.

Does your CV reflect your attributes (education, qualifications, skills and experience) at their best? If not then revise and rewrite it till it does.

Summary
- the job of a CV is to get you an interview with the recruiter
- your CV is your vendor, your advocate- is it your best?
- think carefully of what to include or exclude from the CV
- present yourself as a competent, skilled individual -with a career (skills, experience), and a life (interests, hobbies)
- use active words, write in the recruiter's language
- write a focused, clear, concise and simple CV
- give examples of your success and achievements
- be prepared to discuss, and verify statements in your CV?
- explain gaps in your career (courses, holidays, sickness?..) otherwise they may think you are hiding something
- choose your referees carefully; get their permission
- prepare and send a fresh CV for every application
- update your CV regularly- you may need it sooner!

Further Reading

1 *Peel M.* **Improving Your Communication Skills.** *(Kogan Page 1995*

2 *Corfield R.* **Preparing Your CV** -How to Improve Your Chances of Getting the Job You Want. *(Kogan Page 1990).*

3 *Greenbury LR.* **Portable Careers** -Surviving Your Partner's Relocation. *(Kogan Page 1992).*

4 *Eggert, M.* **The Perfect CV.** *Arrow Business Books 1993*

5 **How to Write a Curriculum Vitae.** [Authors: R Hughes, M Baldwin. D Mortimer].*University of London Careers Service 1994.*

5 Making Applications

5 Making Applications

5.1 Need for applications

With adulthood comes the opportunity to do your own thing, to be your own boss. No more school timetables, school teachers or prefects.

No more school fees -no pocket money either. You *will have to pay your bills -house rent, food, drink, clothes, transport, further training, entertainment -everything.*

Have you learnt how to apply *(request)* for what you want? If nobody taught you, it is not too late. You can learn. It is easy. You have read my notes on setting goals, and analysing jobs and courses. Then the question was -*Is this the right job (course) for me?*

When you apply for a job, an educational placement, or a bank loan, the question asked about you is -*Is this the right candidate?*
- is he suitable for the course?
- is she what we need for the job?
- is he credit worthy (will he repay the loan)?

Ensure that your application works for you. Present yourself as the answer to their needs. Help them conclude that: *This is the right candidate.*

- *How do you make yourself the right candidate?*
- *How can you be the answer to their needs?*

Study their needs before you make the application:
- what do they do?
- what would my duties be if I got the position?
- am I suitable for the position?
- How can I convince them so?

Study the advertisement, if there is one. Talk to people in the institution or occupation you wish to join.
- What do they do?
- What is it like working there?
- Is this what you want to do?
- Is this your future?

Look at your qualifications, experience and skills.
- Are they relevant to the position?
- Is this what you want; do you need it?
- Is this the best you can do?

Now you are ready to *think about making the application.*

5.2 Sources of Information
Use all available sources of information when searching for openings:
- career advisors
- libraries and librarians
- employment agencies
- advertisements in the press
- special publications
- job fairs and recruitment drives
- employment services
- company directories and registers
- college and universities prospectuses
- networking

5.2.1 *Career advisors* at school, college, or your place of work (placement officers after redundancies), can be helpful. Career advisors should have books, and directories for you to consult.

5.2.2 *The Library and librarians* in your school, college, university or town are a mine of useful information and guidance. Exploit the mine for your benefit. Many libraries stock Yellow Pages, Directories, Yearbooks, etc. Ask the librarian. She/he will show you where to look.

5.2.3 *Employment agencies/ consultants* will help you find a job (of course they charge you or your future employer for the service). They may help you to make your CV more presentable. Make sure they have full information on your skills, qualifications, and experience; and the job and pay you want.

Consult the following publications for names of relevant agencies:
- The Yellow Pages
- The Directory of Trainer Support Services
- Yearbook of Recruitment and Employment Services
- The British Medical Journal (for doctors in Britain)
- Nursing Times (for Nurses), etc.

You may have to register with a selection of agencies who would put your name forward and keep you informed of suitable positions.

5.2.4 *Recruitment advertisements* in newspapers, and magazines:
- *General papers* -Financial Times, Daily Telegraph, Guardian, Sunday Times, Daily Express, Independent, Daily Mail, etc.
- *Professional journals* -British Medical Journal, Nursing Times, etc.

5.2.5 *Specialist Publications* aimed at graduates include:
- Graduate Careers & Career Adviser *(Dominion Press)*
- Graduate Scientist and Engineer *(Dominion Press)*
- Register of Graduate Employment and Training *(ROGET)*
- Directory of Opportunities for Graduates *(Newpoint Publications)*.

You careers' officer will usually have copies of these and other publications.

5.2.6 *Job fairs, Recruitment drives* are usually aimed at graduates. You should work out what jobs and professions you want before approaching any company. You want to be recruited by the company you really like.

5.2.7 *Employment (labour) services* (labour offices) may be organised by the Department of Employment/ Ministry of Labour or some other agency. In Britain there are client advisors in Job Centres or Unemployment Benefit Offices. They organise job review workshops, job search seminars, and job clubs to help job seekers.

5.2.8 *Company Registers and directories* will tell you the company size, what it does, how profitable it is. British examples include:
- Guide to British Enterprise *(Dunn and Broadstreet)*
- Who Own Whom *(Dunn and Broadstreet)*
- Times 1000 Leading Companies *(Times Newspapers Ltd)*
- Britain's Top 2000 Private Companies/Britain's Second 2000 Companies *(Jordan Information Services)*
- Kompass Register *(Kompass Publications)*
- Municipal Yearbook and Public Services Directory.   *etc.*

What are the equivalent publications in your country?

5.2.9 *Higher training courses* may be found in university prospectuses in your library. You should write to the college or university for a copy of their current prospectus.

The following two publications have a comprehensive listing of British institutions and the courses on offer:

- British Qualifications *(Kogan Page)*
- British Universities Guide to Graduate Study *(Association of Commonwealth Universities)*.

Similar publications exist in other countries. Can you find yours?.

5.2.10 *Networking/ word of mouth*
Friends or other contacts will have information about jobs/vacancies. Ask your colleagues to tell you of interesting jobs they hear about. Develop a network of people who will tell you of coming openings. This is called *networking*.

5.3 Application forms
Some schools, colleges, companies, banks and other organisations insist on applicants completing standard form(s). Obtain and complete the form carefully, and neatly. It is best to use black ink. If your handwriting is poor, then write in clear CAPITALS. Typed answers (if possible) would be better.

Answer all the questions. Do not write *"Please See CV"* on the form- it is not acceptable and may cause your application to be rejected. You can write *"Please Refer to CV for details"* if the space is not enough- but the summary must be on the form.

The employer requires you to fill in the form. If you want the job fill in the form. Simple!

Organise your information before completing the form. Some applicants practice on a photocopy of the form before completing the original. If asked to complete the form in your handwriting, make sure you are in position to write well (pen, furniture, mood, lighting, posture). Have you heard about character analysis from handwriting?

Be ready to discuss the information you give in the application if called for interview.

5.4 Do they want a CV ?
Do you have a current well written, typed curriculum vitae? If not then read Chapter 4 *(Write your curriculum vitae).*

If asked to send a CV, then send a clean well written current CV. If your CV is out of date, revise it. Rewrite it to meet the needs of the vacancy. Different aspects of your qualifications, experience, and skills may need stressing.

Do not send a tattered and irrelevant CV. It will not be your best advocate, unless you do not wish to be selected! If you are actively looking for a job, you should keep clean copies of your CV for emergencies.

5.5 Is a CV alone enough?
Alone the CV is not enough. It needs a relevant covering letter. The covering letter may be hand-written. If your handwriting is untidy, then type the covering letter too, but sign it in your hand.

5.6 Is a letter good enough?
An ordinary letter is not enough. There should always be a CV, and a covering letter.

Mutindo, a geography graduate applies for a teaching job abroad:

Entebbe High School,
PO Box 66x
Entebbe, Uganda

24 July 1994

The Permanent Secretary
Ministry of Education
PO Maseru, Lesotho.

Dear Sir,

I wish to apply for a job as a geography teacher. I am a 31 year old Ugandan university graduate with a BA (Honours) degree in geography. I have taught geography at Entebbe High School in Uganda for 3 years.

I am a hard working teacher and would be useful in one of your secondary schools.

Yours faithfully,

Michael D Mutindo

MICHAEL D. MUTINDO

Michael`s Application failed to provide vital information:
- what is his education and qualifications?
- how long has he been in teaching (3 years)?
- what does he do outside teaching?
- who are his referees?

In a CV you can give a detailed summary of your career -listing information that would make a letter rather long and boring. What looks right and proper in a CV may look out of place in a letter. Application by CV and covering letter is the standard practice (unless an application form is provided).

5.7 The covering letter

A short well composed and typed letter should accompany every application by CV or by application form. The job of the covering letter is induce the recruiter to read your CV and invite you for interview.

● *Direct it to a named individual or officer* responsible for recruitment. Find out the name of the person, or title of the officer concerned and address your letter to him or her personally. You may have to telephone the organisation to get the names. If getting a job is important to you then get the recruiter's name.

● *Name the post or course* you are applying for and *quote the reference number*. Reference numbers are often included in the advertisement. This ensures that your application goes to the right office and officer. The office may be recruiting for several different jobs (or courses) at the same time. If your application is misdirected or lost you will not be selected.

● *State concisely why you are the right person* for the position (your qualifications, experience, skills and achievements).

● *Write (talk) in the style* appropriate to the recruiter's professional, business, or academic discipline.

● Indicate that you would be interested in discussing the subject further.

- *End* with Yours sincerely *(letter to named person),*
  or Yours faithfully *(no individual named),*
  Sign, and *print your name.*

Alice applied for senior job with the following letter and a CV

Bombo High School
P O Box 77x, Bombo

30 September 1995

Mr S Mfundishi
Chief School Inspector
Ministry of Education
PO Box 7063, Kampala.

Dear Mr Mfundishi

Re: Post of School Inspector (biology teaching)

Biology is an important school subject, and its teaching should be maintained and improved.

My teaching experience, research and publications have given me the skills essential in an effective inspector for biology teaching.

I have taught biology for 21 years have examined at Ordinary and Advanced levels for 17 years. My *Basic Human Biology* is popular with students and teachers.

My CV is enclosed. I look forward to hearing from you.

Yours sincerely,
Alice Awino
ALICE AWINO, BSc MSc
Senior school biology examiner.

5.8 Speculative approaches

You could write to a potential employer and offer your services on the assumption that there is a suitable vacancy. If a vacancy exists you would be considered without competition.

Campbell House
Uganda Martyrs University
PO Box 5498, Kampala.

12 December 1995

Mr Z Katuhe
Managing Director
Beihireyo Books
PO Box 9959, Kampala

Dear Mr Katuhe

Re: Inquiry about the post of Marketing Assistant.

Beihireyo Books are popular with students at this university. I have followed the products and growth of the company with interest. Your company needs people who will contribute to its future success.

I will get my Bachelor of Business Administration (BBA) degree in June 1996. My majors are Marketing, Communications and Accounting. I hope to work in Marketing the publishing industry.

My curriculum vitae is enclosed. I am ready to come to your office to discuss openings in your Marketing department.

Yours sincerely
BKatete
Besiima Katete

It will be more fruitful to directly contact the head of the service or department you wish to work in than sending a blind application to Personnel (Human Resources) Officers. Departmental head know their needs well before personnel officers get to hear about them.

- Write to companies likely to have openings for an individual with your skills and qualifications.

- Direct your application to a named person. Dear Sir/Madam is an insult. It says you are not that much interested in their company. Why should they bother to answer your inquiry?

- Send a letter and a suitable career summary (or CV).

- Make it clear that you will telephone (after a suitable interval) to inquire about their reaction to you inquiry.

5.9 Testimonials

Testimonials are commendations (references) that a candidate keeps with her and may send off with a CV or a completed application form.

Few prospective employers ask for or accept testimonials as references. They prefer to contact your referees confidentially. Testimonials have less influence than confidential references. (Naturally nobody sends out bad testimonials!)

Often references are obtained by telephone or facsimile. So ensure that you have included your referees' telephone and fax numbers. This enables the recruiter to get your reference quickly (in minutes rather than days).

5.10 Applying for sponsorship

Scholarships are in great demand. Because scholarships have in the past been offered as packages *(Z has scholarships for Y courses)*, many students (and parents) expect sponsors to and *find them money and places* for courses. Why should a sponsor get you college *and* pay your college fees? He/ She is not your grandmother!

How can you help a potential sponsor? Let us eavesdrop on the chairman of a scholarship committee somewhere in Sponsorland. Two letters requesting sponsorships were put on his desk on the same day. Listen to his reaction as he reads them.

(Letter A) ...I am interested in studying for a masters degree in Economics. I would be grateful for any help you can give me... Yours faithfully...

(Lazy. Can`t get himself a college place? Send him a booklet on courses.)

(Letter B)....I would like to study for a masters degree in Economics. I enclose a copy of a conditional offer of a place at the London School of Economics for September... I have to show evidence of sponsorship by June.... Yours faithfully....

(Good. Got herself a place at the LSE? Could help here. Recommend to committee next month.)

Do you get the message?
- There are many sources of information on scholarships and sponsors. Public libraries, government ministries and departments, universities, etc. Get yourself informed!
- Occasionally embassies and high commissions (in developing countries) have scholarships. Keep in touch with their information or education offices.

MAKING APPLICATIONS

- Apply to colleges or universities that offer the course you want and obtain a letter offering, or promising you a place.
- Then apply to potential sponsors enclosing a copy of the offer of a place on the course for which you require sponsorship.

Send your applications early. It takes many months to secure a university place or sponsorship. You should apply well before the course you want starts. It may take more than a year!

Your application (by CV and covering letter) should state:
- who you are (names, nationality, qualifications, occupation)
- the course you wish to take, and why you need it
- the duration of the course
- what you intend to do after the course
- the assistance you need (fees, top up grant, subsistence, etc.)?

Also send supportive evidence (*copies of* letter of admission or conditional offer, certificates). *Do not send the originals documents unless specifically asked.* Your prized certificate could get lost. You will take original documents with you if called for interview.

Even if you do not succeed at least you will have done your best.

Summary

Written applications may be made by either:
- a neat, typed, relevant (CV), and a Covering Letter; or
- a completed application form, *(type, or use black ink)* and a Covering Letter; or
- a speculative letter and a career summary (CV).

Sometimes a completed application form and a CV are needed.

Your application should arrive before the closing date.

Further reading

1 **Leeds, Dorothy.** Marketing Yourself *How to sell yourself and get the jobs you've always wanted. (Piatkus 1991)*

2 **Carnegie, Dale.** How to Win Friends and Influence People. *Cedar 1981*

3 **Peel, M.** Improving Your Communication Skills. *(Kogan Page 1995*

4 **Greenbury, LR.** Portable Careers -Surviving Your Partner's Relocation. *(Kogan Page 1992).*

5 **Wholey, John.** The Small Business Action Kit. *(Kogan Page 1994)*

6 The Grants Register. *(Macmillan)*

6 Taking Interviews

6 Taking Interviews

6.1 What is an interview?

An interview is the occasion when a candidate (interviewee) is seen (viewed) and questioned by interviewer(s) to determine her suitability for the services or privilege she seeks.

6.2 What are interviews for?

Several candidates may be short listed and interviewed to select the most suitable. A sole applicant would not be appointed if he were unsuitable for the post. The search then continues. The question is: *Is this candidate suitable? A candidate may have the diplomas and years of experience but still be unsuitable for the post.*

Is he the right person for the job?

Does he have the right qualifications, experience, skills and personality? Is this the right job for his qualifications and skills? Sometimes a candidate may not be appointed because the interviewer thinks he would be better employed in a different capacity.

Is he suitable for the course?

Does he have the entry qualifications, the aptitude and stamina to finish the course? Will he benefit from the course? Does he need this course?

Sometimes a candidate may be refused a post because too many candidates of his kind have already been accepted. A candidate with inferior qualifications may be preferred for geographical, ethnic, sex, or religious considerations.

Is he a suitable client?
A request for a favour or service (bank loan, membership of a group, shop credit, etc.) may be refused after interviewing the applicant. Then the question was:

- will she repay the loan?
- will she return my dress?
- is he suitable for our club?
- will she manage the payments?

etc.

Often critical decisions (yes-no, trust-distrust, love-hate, good-bad etc.) are made after brief encounters (*interviews*). You meet him and in a few moments, you dislike him. He has failed the interview!

Normally only candidates with the right qualifications are invited for interview. So it is not lack of qualifications but rather the *impression* you create by your *Appearance, Speech, Confidence*, and *Personality* that determines your suitability.

Interviews are about *impressions.* Create a good impression and you may get what you asked for. Create a poor impression and your application will fail.

6.3 Preparing for interview
Before the interview find out as much as possible about the post and organisation.

- What do they do?
- What would I be doing?
- What is the course about?
- Is it an exciting place to work/study at?

etc.

You will be seen and questioned. Do you have any questions? *Take your certificates, CV, Identification*, and other relevant documents with you. The interviewer may want to see them.

Are you ready to discuss your education, work experiences, and hobbies smoothly and confidently? It would be a shame if you did not remember the contents of your CV. Study a copy of the CV you sent with the application. Read the job and person specification again to ensure that your answers are accurate and relevant.

Let us list a few questions commonly asked at interviews. Think about sensible answers to these and many others.

Job Interviews
- Why did you apply for this job?
- What were your main duties in your last job?
- What do you do particularly well?
- What are your main weaknesses?
- What are your main strengths?
- Why did you leave your last employer?
- What are your career objectives?
- Why should we employ you?   etc.

Interviews for educational courses
- Why do you wish to take this course?
- Have you applied to other courses?
- What will you do after the course?
- How will you pay for the course?
- What will you live on?   etc.

Interviews for loans (bank, society, etc)

- Why do you want the money?
- What is your income and expenses?
- What other sources of finance do you have?
- Do you have other financial commitments?
- What security do you offer ?
- Have you ever been refused a loan?
- How do you intend to repay the loan?   etc.

Do you have any questions?

Sometimes interviewers ask if the candidate has any questions. After thinking of possible answers to common interview questions, you should think of some questions you would like to ask the panel. You may be told the salary and other benefits during the interview. Remember these facts. It will not be impressive to ask questions whose answers have just been given to you. You do not have to ask questions, but do ask if something is not clear.

Do you have questions about training, changing jobs within the organisation, criteria and opportunities for promotion? Do not ask irrelevant questions.

6.4 Pre-interview visits

Employment candidates are encouraged to visit the prospective place of work before the interview. Whenever possible visit before sending an application. During the visit you should:

- look over as much of the institution as possible
- speak to individuals you would be working with or at the level of your planned employment and to more junior workers
- speak to management and see the chief executive if you are seeking a senior position.
- ask questions and listen to the answers and explanations
- discuss you duties: what will the employer expect of you?

This is the time for you to ask questions and satisfy yourself that:
- you like the place, the people, and the prospective job
- you understand what is expected of you in the job
- the rewards will be adequate and appropriate for the work done.

Sometimes several visits are needed to satisfy yourself that this is the job for you. You should telephone the contact person or other senior official and other workers for information and clarifications if you need them. If you take a bad job, it is difficult to move to another- *Why are you leaving your current employer?* This is the question you don't need to answer repeatedly.

6.5 Presenting yourself for interview
You are mentally ready. You have your certificates, identity and invitation to the interview. What have you forgotten?

What will you look like (appearance, confidence, personality); sound like (voice, language, knowledge, confidence, personality)?

Appearance
Your appearance will contribute to your performance at the interview. You should wear suitable, smart, and clean clothes. These should be items you are comfortable in. Do not wear clothes that make you uncomfortable. If you are uncomfortable your performance and the impression you create will be poor.

I usually wear my best and most comfortable trousers, shirt, jacket and shoes. I talk better if I am not being strangled by a tight collar, squeezed by a jacket too small for my chest, or a pair of trousers that threatens to split into two each time I shift my buttocks.

Wear clothes that suit the position you seek. Think of the age and possible bias of the interviewers and wear clothes that are unlikely to offend their sense of propriety. Some types of clothing are not generally acceptable (irrespective of quality):

- an ordinary shirt is more acceptable that a T-shirt.
- jeans are unacceptable; wear ordinary trousers.
- trousers worn by female candidates may not yet be acceptable to traditional (conservative?) interviewers. Smart traditional female clothes may be safer.
- good quality skirts and jackets are fashionable (and acceptable) for female candidates particularly those seeking management positions, and senior professional jobs.
- it may be safer to wear little or no jewellery than to carry inappropriate metal!

Is your hair groomed, your fingernails clean and trimmed, your shoes shined and in good repair? Have you had a bath? It would be a shame if you offended the interviewer's nose.

I know very little about perfumes; but if I were the interviewer I would not be favourably impressed by some candidate who smelt like a perfume factory. Use light perfume, and only if you normally use the stuff and know what is good and what is not!

Politeness
On arrival at the place of interview speak and make your inquiries politely. You never know who is looking and listening. Do not offend any body. You may meet them again in the interview room! Worse still the gentleman or lady at reception may be the boss. It has happened before.

Frank was invited to an interview for a job as an Accounts Clerk in as small but expanding bookshop. At reception he found an elderly lady busy typing.
"Can I help you, Sir?" inquired the lady looking at the smartly dressed young man.

"Yes you can. I have come for an interview" Frank replied.
"Ah. Take a seat please. I will be with you in a moment. Let me first
finish this letter. I paid for some books from India 4 months ago.
They were to be sent to Entebbe by air-freight. Nothing has arrived
at the airport yet!"

The lady continued typing her letter. She referred to files and ledger
books several times. As she was about to pull the page out of the
typewriter, she heard an impatient cough from Frank and looked at
him. He was standing, briefcase in hand, glaring at her.
"I had an appointment for interview here ten minutes ago. What
is going on?" he demanded.
"Wait. I will be with you in a few minutes". She pulled the letter out
of the typewriter, folded it and put it into an envelope. She stood up
and looked at Frank eye-to-eye. He was still glaring at her. He did
not recognise her as the boss. He only saw a typist.

"You may leave now. Your interview is over, Sir", the shopkeeper
said. Frank hesitated for a moment and then walked out.

Bosses do not have to be behind big desks before they start
interviewing you. Remain alert and listen. You may not be warned
that the interview has began. What matters is not the grandeur of the
setting but the impression you make in the interviewer's mind.

Kiberu, an accountant, told me a nice story about an interview he
had a few years ago. On his way to the interview he shared a lift
with a man and a woman. The man asked him where he was going.
Kiberu said he was on his to an interview for a job with a company
on the 10th floor. They chatted about his education and
qualifications and what he had done in the past. He even talked
about his ambition of becoming a chartered accountant. When the
lift stopped at the 10th floor, the man and woman got out too. They
entered the office with Kiberu. They proceeded into an inner room,
leaving him at reception. After about five minutes the secretary was

asked to send in the candidate. Kiberu was shown into the inner office.

"I am Milumbi. This is Mrs Ogwang; and that is Mr Nkombe. You haven`t met him yet. He is the third member of the panel. Mrs Ogwang and I have told him about our conversation in the lift. You told us all we need for the interview, and very well too".
"Thank you, Sir."
"May I look at your certificates please?" Mr Nkombe requested.

Kiberu handed his certificates and identity card to Mr Nkombe, who examined and returned them. He nodded his approval. They talked about salary, a car loan, and when he would start work; then he was asked to wait in reception for a while. Half an hour later he was given a letter of appointment.

When you enter the interview room wait till asked to sit. Then sit on the chair so that you are comfortable. Do not sit on the edge of the chair and risk falling off! Sit up, and remain attentive. You should not sit as if you own the place. Look at each member of the panel as they are introduced to you. Remember their names. You may have to ask them questions later.

Speech

We speak to convey information, to be understood. So when you answer questions, **speak so that your answer is heard clearly and understood.** You should neither whisper nor shout. Watch the interviewers to see if they hear you well and understand your answers. Your purpose is to convince the panel of your suitability. If they cannot hear you well, they will not know how good you are. Look at the interviewer eye-to-eye for brief moments. Move your attention to the person speaking to you and listen. Understand the question before answering it. If it is not clear, ask him or her to explain. **Speak clearly, concisely, and simply.**

Do not use jargon or abbreviations unless you are certain your interviewer knows them too. Use ordinary words and language, and give full words unless the abbreviation is common knowledge. Use your best language. *Be clear, brief, and informative in your answers.* Answer the question asked.

Give your answers politely but confidently. You should be sure of your answers because you prepared for the interview. If you do not know say so clearly and confidently too. You will not get any credit for pretending to know.

If an interviewer is talking do not interrupt. Let him talk. Listen and be ready to answer the question that is sure to follow the speech.

During the interview:
- Do not sit till invited - or until the interviewer sits
- Do not draw attention to your weaknesses
- Do not criticise your previous employer
- Do not constantly repeat questions
- Do not smoke even if invited to
- Do not interrupt the interviewer
- Do not argue with the interviewer
- Do not get too familiar or personal
- Control your distracting mannerisms
- Smile- it is allowed; laughing is taboo
- Do tell the truth- it is easier to talk about
- Look at the interviewer, use his/her name
- Speak clearly, succinctly, give full answers.

Confidence, Personality, body language
Your confidence and personality will be judged from your
appearance, dress, composure, mannerisms, and speech. Your
confidence is improved by your knowledge and preparedness. You
portray your best personality if you are well dressed, polite, and
speak clearly and audibly.

Avoid annoying mannerisms [picking your nose, yawning, clicking
your knuckles, constantly clearing your throat, etc.].

6.6 Questions about past failures
Sometimes candidates are asked to talk about important past failures.
Be prepared to talk about some of your past failures. Talk about
failures whose cause was identified, lessons learnt and which you are
now able to talk about calmly and rationally.

Conclusion
You will be interviewed and will interview others for most of your
(working and retired) life. So cultivate a manner of dress,
demeanour, and speech that says *-he (she) is reliable, capable,
trustworthy, an achiever.*

It takes time to develop a reliable, capable, hardworking and
confident personality. You have the time. Use it well.

Summary
- is this the right job, do you need this interview?
- did you visit the place, have you met the people?
- are your mentally ready (questions on skills, past work...)
- are you physically prepared *(dress, bearing, speech...)*
- do you have the appropriate documentation?
- are you satisfied about the job and rewards?
- relax and do your best

Further reading

1. *Leeds, Dorothy.* **Marketing Yourself** *How to sell yourself and get the jobs you've always wanted. Piatkus 1991.*

2 *Spillane, Mary.* **Presenting Yourself** - *a Personal Image Guide for Women. Piatkus 1993.*

3 *Spillane, Mary.* **Presenting Yourself** - *a Personal Image Guide for Men. Piatkus 1993.*

4 *Brown, M. Brandreth G.* **How to Interview and be Interviewed.** *Sheldon Press 1986.*

When is your next interview?

7 Writing Research Papers

7 Writing research papers

7.1 What is research?

To me research means *searching again* for an insight, an answer, a solution to an important, or intriguing question or problem. Research is more than basic reading and looking for information from books, journal or magazine.

Information should be gathered, and ordered so that the problems can be better defined. Frequently one finds the answer at this level. This is basic reading and not research. To *re*search you should have finished the basic search.

7.2 Requirements for research

- An intriguing or important problem
- An intrigued or challenged mind
- Basic intelligence, diligence, interest in finding out
- Resources (material, money, time, and space).

The most import item is an intriguing or challenging problem. Without the challenge it is difficult to sustain a research effort. The desire to solve a problem helps in looking for resources - time, space, and money (personal savings, seeking grants from individuals and public bodies).

7.3 Planning Research

Many students ask for help in doing research before identifying the challenge they wish to pursue, the problem that must be solved.

James Mukasa had to write a dissertation for his MSc in Education
course. He went to Mr Kilevu, his tutor for help.

"What will your dissertation be about?" the tutor asked.
"I don't know yet. I hope you can help me."
"Have you identified any problem you wish to study for your
dissertation?"
"No, Sir. I was hoping you would advise me", replied Mukasa.
"Help you do what? Talk with teachers at Katwe Primary School
You know them. What are the educational problems in the school,
among teachers, pupils, parents?"
"I don't know where to start", replied Mukasa.
"Come back on Friday with a few ideas. Then we can talk".

Mukasa was annoyed by his tutor's attitude. He left the office
mattering curses and headed for the library. He met Alice Awino, a
fellow student on the course, walking away from the library.
"What is the problem? Why are you so annoyed", Alice asked.
"I went to Kilevu to talk about my dissertation. He would not help
me. He said I should ask school teachers in Katwe!".

"Mr Kilevu is the best tutor on writing dissertations. He does not do
it for you. He helps you learn how to do it. I was at Katwe Primary
School last week. Now I am researching why Baganda pupils from
Katwe do not do as well as those from Kololo",
"What did Kilevu do for you then?"
"He asked me how I would measure 'doing well', and through
questions guided me to simple, but fairly good measures of home
circumstances, (foods availability books at home, father's work,
parental ambition for the child), growth of pupils (height and
weight) and of school performance. (P7 exam pass rates), and
others", replied Alice.

"Is that what they are paid to do?", asked James.
"They are employed to help you learn. I think I am learning from Mr Kilevu. See you tomorrow."

James went into the library. He selected a book on sociological research methods from a self. It was hard reading. His mind drifted and he thought about his home, his parents and brothers and his sisters in-law and their children. Nambi's children were thriving. Nakate's were malnourished, one had died of kwashiorkor. Nakate had finished P7. Nambi had never been to school.

"Most children dying of kwashiorkor belong to 'semi-educated' mothers. Why?"

Mukasa went back to his tutor's office to ask if he could see him the following day.
"I have a free 30minutes. Alice has cancelled her appointment. She wants to collect more data first. How can I help you?"

They talked about child nutrition, brain growth and educational performance. Mr Kilevu helped Mukasa to define the subject of his dissertation. Mukasa read sociological and medical books and journals on infant malnutrition. Then he went to his village conduct his study.

Mukasa and Awino would write good dissertations. Mr Kilevu would be happy to have helped them learn a little about research.

Planning research of course means more than getting ideas. What needs to be done depends on the research problem.

Research on humans and animals *requires **approval*** from control bodies. Studies involving ***humans*** usually require ***informed consent*** from the individual (or somebody acting for him/her) ***before*** the study starts.

7.4 Doing research

Details of research are beyond the remit of "Write them Right". If you must then consult a good library, and the nearest research department that does work in your field of interest.

Does your research require:
- laboratory experiments (equipment, materials, assistants)?
- interviewing many people (assistants, questionnaires)?
- a study of old books and manuscripts (access to rare books)?
- human patients- informed consent (confidentiality, ethics)?
- data from private and public business (confidentiality, security)?

These and many other issues must be considered and resolved before the actual study begins.

Fortunately most studies by students are not so involved. Simple politeness, and humility when asking people to do things for you is important particularly in sociological and medical studies.

After discussing his interest in infant malnutrition and maternal education with his tutor, Mukasa was able to work out a plan for his study.

He went back to his home gombolola. He talked with the chief. He visited the local health department and talked with senior nurses and doctors. He enlisted the help of the health visitor and paediatrician in identifying and counting true kwashiorkor. He talked with teachers in local schools; and with elderly men and women who remembered child rearing before 'education and schools.'

- *He interviewed*
  - *mothers about their educational attainments, literacy in Luganda, and English.*
  - *mothers with normal children and those whose chidden had kwashiorkor.*

- *He observed feeding practices in families with normal children and in those with malnourished children*
- *With the help of the health visitor, he recorded details of children with kwashiorkor.*
- *He inquired about how mothers and fathers spent their money.*
- *He inquired about changes in child rearing methods.*

- *He carefully recorded his findings- [two A4 pages per mother].*

In 4 weeks he collected detailed information on 457 mothers and their children. His mother remarked that she had never seen him so concerned and involved with babies. "When will you marry and get your own?"

After collecting his data, Mukasa thanked everybody who had helped him and returned to the university to analyse the data and write his dissertation.

7.5 Analysing data

On returning to Kampala, Mukasa discussed the conduct of his study and the data with his tutor. Mr Kilevu was impressed with Mukasa's field work.

Was kwashiorkor and maternal education related?
Mukasa collated and tabulated the data into simple categories.
- *Maternal age (years): 15-20, 21-25, 26-30, over 30.*
- *Maternal education: None, P1-P4, P5-7, S1-2, S3-4, GCE+*
- *Nutritional state: Normal, -Doubtful, -Definite kwashiorkor*

He calculated and related the rates kwashiorkor to maternal age education, and village of residence.

One aspect of his study, changes in infant rearing was difficult to quantify. However he had listened to elderly women and men and made notes. The quotes were illuminating.

Some research findings are easy to quantify others are not. Often sociological, cultural and historical studies are more interesting when recorded and reported as qualitative (flavour) rather than quantitative trends. The style of reporting depends on the primary question.

7.6 Writing the paper

Research papers usually follow a standard format: *introduction, methods, results, conclusion . (See examples in your library)*.

However important discoveries have been reported as letters to editors of journals. The structure of deoxyribonucleic acid (DNA), the genetic code, was reported by Watson and Crick in a letter to *The Lancet*, a British medical journal.

How should Mukasa write up the findings of his study?.
"You have done well. Your data is interesting, " Mr Kilevu told him after examining the analysis of the study.
"Thank you. It was exciting. There are so many questions I wanted to ask those women. Why do they.. ", Mukasa bubbled.
"Slow down James. One step at a time. First your dissertation, an MSc and then you can go back and ask your questions!

Perhaps we could do something substantial with your study. Gives me a chance to show you something not frequently done with students here".
"What is that? Asked Mukasa suspiciously.
"It is simple really. Your data could be written up as a paper for a journal. I can think of three -in education, sociology, medicine- that could be interested -if the paper was well written. "

"But I only have two months to finish the dissertation". Mukasa objected.

"Ah well. It was a thought. It would have been a double coup. Two birds with one stone," murmured Kilevu.

Mukasa did not understand the 'double coup and two birds' bit, and kept quiet. They discussed the structure and style of the dissertation, and Mukasa left.

Mukasa found Alice in the canteen eating her dinner. He recounted the tutor's reaction to the analysis of his study.

"What would have been a double coup- two birds with one stone?", Mukasa asked Alice.

"A published research paper and an MSc dissertation, stupid"

Mukasa frowned and Alice thought she had gone too far with the 'stupid' thing. Some of the men were sensitive to remarks like that from female students. Then Mukasa smiled and Alice felt better.

"Thanks Miss Awino. I owe you a drink. But how do you write a research paper?"

"It's simple really: Introduction, Methods, Results, Discussion, Conclusion and, Recommendations- just like a dissertation, but more concise and focused," replied Alice showing off. Mr Kilevu had that morning, persuaded her to write a paper based on her study. She was excited.

"God bless your brains. Let us go for the drink before I remember the state of my finances," replied Mukasa.

They finished their dinner and moved to the drinks bar. Mukasa bought her a beer, and a double Waragi for himself. They were getting fond of each other.

7.6.1 The title

The title should encapsulate the subject and the findings of the study. It should be short, relevant, informative, and memorable. *E.g:*

Mother's Education and Kwashiorkor

7.6.2 Abstract/ Summary

Though it follows the title, the abstract is written last. It gives a summary of the purpose, methods, findings and conclusions of the study. Many readers start and finish with the abstract. It should reflect the essence of the paper *(see example on next page).*

Subheadings make abstracts easier to read. Often the abstract is one solid paragraph.

7.6.3 Introduction

o Why was the study done? What were you looking for?

Mukasa was intrigued by the apparent excess of deaths and morbidity from kwashiorkor among children of semi-educated women in his gombolola. By doing the study he will discover if it is really true or if his impressions are clouded by the fate of his nephews and nieces. His introduction to the paper should say so and need not be bigger than this paragraph. He may cite a few published studies on the same or related topics.

7.6.4 Methods (including subjects and materials)

● What did you study (subjects,)? *He studied the association of kwashiorkor and maternal education.*
● What did you do? *He gathered data on maternal education and the incidence of kwashiorkor in their children*
● How did you do it? *He interviewed mothers, and elders in a community and recorded information on child rearing.*

111

Mukasa wrote the following abstract for his paper.

Mother's education and kwashiorkor

James Mukasa, Makerere Institute of Education, Kampala.

ABSTRACT

Objective
To delineate the relationship between maternal education and the incidence of kwashiorkor.

Subjects and methods
457 mothers and their children in 6 hamlets in Luwero and were studied. Elders were interviewed on parenting and infant care.

Findings
There is was a complex relationship between maternal education and kwashiorkor. Kwashiorkor was high in children of poorly educated mothers, and low in those of uneducated and well educated mothers. Kwashiorkor was higher in children of women born in certain villages.

Conclusions
Mis-education and mother's upbringing are associated with infant malnutrition. Good education is protective.

7.6.5 Results (findings)
- What did you find? *What did Mukasa's analysis reveal?.*
- Did you find any gems? *Any unusual findings?*

Mukasa found that the relationship of kwashiorkor to maternal education was not simple. Many semi-educated woman fed their children better as they gained more experience. Some did not learn and their children continued to suffer. Some families had no malnourished children irrespective of maternal education

His paper included the tabulated incidence (numbers and percentages) of kwashiorkor in the various categories -maternal age, education and village before marriage. He calculated statistical significance levels when there was a suggestion of association.

Statistics become important with serious studies. They attempt to measure the probability that the findings occurred by chance. Most educational libraries will have books on statistics.

7.6.6 Discussion
- What do the findings mean?
- Were the results worth the trouble?
- How do your findings compare with published studies?
- What were the shortcoming of the study?
- Could you have done this study better? How?

Mukasa's study showed that there was some relationship between maternal education and infantile kwashiorkor. However the association was less noticeable as the mothers aged and had more children. Most of them had learnt from the experience of having a child with kwashiorkor.

Some parts of his community had a lower incidence of kwashiorkor irrespective of maternal education, and in some parishes the risk of kwashiorkor decreased with maternal education. Mukasa's study showed that the quality of education, parental knowledge and parenting skills determine whether a young mother's child will be malnourished or not. Mis-education could be damaging.

Some of Mukasa's findings have been reported before and he will cite published papers in his article (and dissertation).

7.6.7 Conclusions
- What are your conclusions?
- What are the implications of the findings?

Mukasa's study showed that the quality of education is important. Wrong learning could be damaging. Teaching of (skilled, well informed, practical) parenting and child rearing should not be neglected. If the children are at school (not learning in the traditional way) formal education should include parenting skills.

7.6.8 Recommendations
- What should be done next?

Mukasa hopes to study the relationship of schools attended, village of origin, and father's education to infant malnutrition.

7.6.9 References/citations
At the end of a paper (article) for publication in a professional journal, the author gives the details of papers and books he has referred to in the article. I have often wished that popular magazines could do the same. Often I read something in a popular magazine I wish to follow up; but there was no clue. What a pity. See 5.3.5 *(Publications)* for examples on citing references.

Mukasa listed the journals and books cited in his article.

7.7 Writing for magazines

Magazine articles read different and have a different structure from research papers. Writing for popular magazines can be financially rewarding. If you are interested you should read the magazines you want to write for to gain a feel of the style, structure and degree of detail desired.

Magazine articles also have:
- an *introduction*- to capture the readers attention
- a *body*- to give details of the subject or story, and
- and *recommendation* to the reader.

Residential and correspondence courses on most aspects of writing are available in many countries. Your library may have books on writing.

Further Reading

1 Hendreickse RG. *Protein Energy Malnutrition*. In **Paediatrics in the Tropics** (page 119-213). Editors: Hendreickse RG, Barr DGD, Matthews TS. *Blackwell Scientific Publications 1991*.

2 *Calnan J*. **Coping with Research** -The complete Guide for Beginners. *Heinemann, London 1984*.

3 *McNeil P*. **Research Methods**. *Routledge 1990*.

4 *Fink A, Kosecoff J*. **How to Conduct Surveys** -a step-by-step guide. *Sage Publications 1985*

5 *MAlec MA.* **Essential Statistics for Research.** *Westview Press 1993.*

6 *Friedman LM.* **Fundamentals of Clinical Trials.** *Yearbook Medical Publishers Inc. 1996.*

7 *Dick J.* **Writing for Magazines.** *A&C Black 1994.*

8 *Baker D.* *How to Write Stories for Magazines* -a practical guide to how to write, present and sell your stories to a wide range of magazines. *Allison & Busby 1995.*

9 **Writing Magazine.** *-a monthly publication covering most writing styles and genera and other issues.* Writers News Ltd, PO Box 4, Nairn IV12 4HU, Scotland, UK.

10 **Writers' Monthly.** *-a monthly, similar to (4), ?more serious.* Writers' Monthly, 29 Turnpike Lane, London N8 0EP.

8 Dissertations and Theses

Dissertations and theses are similar to research papers; except for the extent of their length, thoroughness and exposition.

The main parts of a dissertation (or thesis) are:
- Introduction *(several pages, a chapter long)*
- Methods *(a few pages)*
- Results/findings *(one to several chapters)*
- Discussion *(several pages, a chapter)*
- Conclusions *(a page or two)*
- Recommendations *(a page or two)*
- References/sources *(several pages)*
- Appendices *(several to many pages).*

While a paper may be a few pages long, a dissertation may be a few hundred pages. Some of the sections may be long enough to need division into chapters. The results section is frequently several chapters long. But a dissertation requires more than length.

The quality of a dissertation is not directly related to its length. Short dissertations can be very good. Length may be a result of excellent research and thorough writing. It could also be attained by unfocused writing and irrelevant detail.

It is the quality of your research, the depth and relevance of your analysis, and the style and language of the writing that matter; not the weight *[lb or kg]* of the *book*.

Written studies for Diplomas and some Masters degree courses are usually called *Dissertations*; while those for most Masters and PhD degrees are *Theses*.

[Ph.D. = philosophy doctor (doctor of philosophy). You don't have to be a philosopher to get it. It is usually awarded after the Masters degree].

[Dissertation = critique, thesis, discourse, essay, exposition, treatise, etc. Thesis = treatise, dissertation, essay, monograph, hypothesis, etc].

Now you know the difference. Me, I am not so sure!

A thesis is supposed to be more thorough than a dissertation. However some dissertations are quite good, sometimes better than some theses. Your university will be happy to send you details of its higher degree programme.

If you are about to write a dissertation or thesis you should go to your college or university library and examine several. Study their:
● structure and layout (format)
● language style, and grammar
● use of tables, figures and quotations
● depth and sophistication of exposition
● finish (production) and quality of the *book.*

Select two you consider the best and read them more closely to get a better feel of a good thesis (dissertation).

When you write your own, do not try to reproduce the language of a particular dissertation or thesis. Write it your way.

What will be the tone of your dissertation/thesis?

- First person singular -
  - *I studied the mating habits of 124 kites,*   Or
- Third person singular
  - ***The author** studied the mating habits of 124 kites....*
  - *The mating habits of 124 kites were studied...*

It is claimed that the *third person singular* encourages objectivity. That is false. One can be as biased in the *third* as in the *first person singular*. I have read quite objective reports and papers where the author(s) used *I* or *We*.

Repeating *"the author"* is tedious when a simple (and humble) "*I*" would suffice.

Fortunately there is a welcome tendency to use the **I** or **We** tone in academic writing. ***Find out the tone your examiners prefer*** and use that. After your (Diploma, BA, BSc, MSc, PhD, etc.), you may then write in the style of your choice.

Further Reading

1 *Calnan J.* **Coping with Research**- The complete Guide for Beginners. *Heinemann, London 1984.*

2 *Luey B.* **Handbook for Academic Authors.** *Cambridge University Press 1990*

3 *Watson G.* **Writing a Thesis** -a guide to long essays and dissertations. *Longman 1987.*

4 *McNeil P.* **Research methods.** *Routledge 1990.*

9 Writing Reports

9 Writing reports

9.1 What is a report?

A report is a document written to communicate the findings (and implications) of an inquiry, study of an incident, phenomenon, or some other problem to another person or persons (who commissioned it).

Before writing the report you should establish
- the purpose of the report
- the audience (who it is aimed at)
- who will read it and who will use it
- what you want to communicate, to achieve, how, and why?

You should also inquire about the audience. You should know:
- their level of education (so as to use appropriate language)
- level of authority (ability to act on the report)
- knowledge of the subject (to judge the pitch of the report)
- attitude towards the subject (what biases to overcome).

9.2 Structure of a report

A report has a structure, a beginning, a middle, and an end.
- an introduction to say what the report is about
- the body where the reader is told what you want her to know
- a summary to tell the reader what you have told her/him.

Published reports have a standard structure -what the reader now expects to find when she opens a *report*. If your report departs too far from this structure, the unusual format may detract from the impact of the findings, and recommendations.

The usual format of a report is:

9.2.1 A Title Page
This shows
- the title
- The author(s') name(s) - [Your name]
- A statement of the subject of the report
- The date (of writing or publication).

9.2.2 The contents list
This should show the full list of sections (or chapters) of the report (including appendices, references etc) and their page numbers.

9.2.3 A Summary
A concise outline of what the report says (in two or three short paragraphs). The summary is usually written last, and in the third person singular. *"This report considered the issue of...."*

9.2.4 An Introduction
This gives a concise explanation of the terms (aims/context) of the report. It should contain succinct details of essential background information to enable the reader to understand the report.

9.2.5 The body of the report
This is where you write the main findings of your report
- it should be based on an analysis of the issues, and findings
- back up what you write with evidence and argument
- make a clear distinction between facts and opinions.

The body should be subdivided into sections (or chapters) if it is long. The sections should be sequentially numbered *(as in this book)* to assist reference to material. Graphs and charts should be used where appropriate.

9.2.6 Conclusions are the judgements (opinions) you have reached after studying the subject. E.g:

"The poor examination results are a consequence of poor teaching and not of the quality of students."

Conclusions should not be confused with recommendations.

9.2.7 Recommendations are the actions your conclusions lead you to believe to be necessary to improve/ redress/ alter the situation.

"All teachers should attend a course on teaching the new school curriculum"

9.2.8 References, bibliography
Give details of the sources cited in your report. E.g:

*Polnay L (chairman). **Health Needs of School Age Children.** British Paediatric Association 1995. ISBN 0-9500491-9-0.*

9.2.9 The Appendices
This is the place for information not essential to the flow of the argument of the report, but which some readers may wish to study.

Further Reading

1 **Peel M.** Improving Your Communication Skills
   (Kogan Page 1995)

2 **Mort S.** Professional Report Writing. *Gower 1992.*

Index